Making Short Films

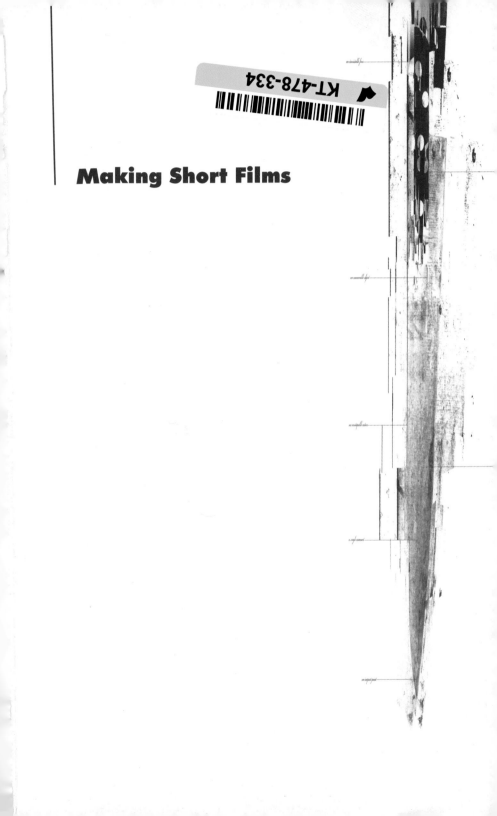

Making Short Films

The Complete Guide from Script to Screen

Clifford Thurlow

Oxford • New York

English edition
First published in 2005 by
Berg
Editorial offices:
First Floor, Angel Court, 81 St Clements Street, Oxford OX4 1AW, UK
175 Fifth Avenue, New York, NY 10010, USA

Berg is the imprint of Oxford International Publishers Ltd.

Library of Congress Cataloging-in-Publication Data
Thurlow, Clifford.
   Making short films : the complete guide from script to screen / Clifford
Thurlow.—English ed.
      p. cm.
   Includes bibliographical references and index.
   ISBN 1-84520-063-2 (pbk.)—ISBN 1-84520-062-4 (cloth)
   1. Short films—Production and direction. 2. Short films—
Authorship. I. Title.
   PN1995.9.P7T49 2005
   791.4302'3—dc22

                                                                    2004028572

British Library Cataloguing-in-Publication Data

A catalogue record for this book is available from the British Library.

ISBN-13   978 1 84520 062 6 (hardback)
               978 1 84520 063 3 (paperback)

ISBN-10   1 84520 062 4 (hardback)
               1 84520 063 2 (paperback)

Typeset by JS Typesetting Ltd, Porthcawl, Mid Glamorgan
Printed in the United Kingdom by Biddles Ltd, King's Lynn

www.bergpublishers.com

For my parents, Clifford and Lilian Thurlow

Contents

Illustrations

Acknowledgments

The aim of this book is to place the short film in its historic context and trace the journey through the process from writing to screening shorts. I am particularly indebted to Sacha Van Spall for compiling the glossary of film terms and festivals' list, as well as reading and making valuable comments on the manuscript. Likewise, many thanks to Iris Gioia and Mike Wallington, for checking my facts, as well as my prose.

There is no film without the script and this book would be incomplete without the screenplays of Terence Doyle, Eoin O'Callaghan and Martin Pickles, who have kindly allowed me to reproduce their work. For insightful comments on directing shorts, and the pleasure being able to study their films, I am grateful to Cedric Behrel, Alexis Bicât, Clive Brill and Dušan Tolmac. Sam Small has initiated me into the arcane world of the editor and from him I have learned that every cut changes nuance and meaning.

Many thanks to the team at the NPA: Yalda Arminian, David Castro and Kevin Dolan; and the help in large and small ways from photographer Cleo Bicât, Juan Luis Buñuel, Andrea Calderwood, Peter Chipping, Breege Collins, Andrew Ellis, Elliot Grove at Raindance, Trish Healy at Empower Training, Petter Hegre and Luba Shumeyko

Hegre, Sally Hibbin, Simon Hinkley, Phil Hunt, Himesh Kar of the Film Council, Elizabeth MacLeod Matthews, Maedhbh McMahon, Tristan Palmer and Hannah Shakespeare at Berg Publishers, Phil Parker, Kevin Phelan, Jack Pizzey, Philip Robertson, Daniel San, Dawn Sharpless at Dazzle Films, Boyd Skinner, Sudie Smyth, Max Thurlow, and my sister Ruth Thurlow, Roger Tooley, Tom Treadwell, Alexis Varouxakis, *webmaster* Jonny White; Tiffany Whittome of Piper Films for her valuable insights on product placement, and Michael Zeffertt for his constant support.

A warm thank you to Maureen Murray, who has taught me how to write (that is re-write) screenplays, and who took me out in the sub-zero January weather to work as an extra on the short film *Room Eleven*. I am indebted to Mark Duffield, for clarifying the technical aspects described in the book. Thanks yet again to Urve Landers for her intuitive comments, and to my mentor, Tudor Gates, for the gift of his time and experience. No book is published without a good editor and I was fortunate indeed to have David Thurlow performing this vital role with extreme diligence. *Greta May* went into production in October 2004 and the following people turned the script into film: Sacha Van Spall, Maureen Murray, Jean-Phillippe Gossart, Renee Willis, Pete Nash, Susan Hodgetts, Pete Carrier, Julian Nagel, John Pearce, Maja Meschede, Sydney Florence, Jenny Spelling, Daniel Rosen, Daniel Owen, Alex Atwater, Max Thurlow, Adam Partridge, Adam Greves, Gerardo Silano, Niccolo Gioia, Nick Burgess and Luc Tremoulet. Thanks finally to my excellent cast: Jess Murphy, Philip Desmueles, Emma Rand, Thomas Snowdon, David Sterne and Tim Pearce.

Writers appreciate feedback, bad as well as good, but better when it's good. The portal is always open at <www.cliffordthurlow. com>

Clifford Thurlow

>> IN THE LONG HOT summer of 1929, Luis Buñuel set out for Cadaqués, an isolated fishing village clinging to the last rocky outcrops of the Pyrenees and inaccessible except by sea. Buñuel carried the first draft of a short film under his arm and was making the journey from Aragon to the Spanish coast to see Salvador Dalí, his collaborator.

They had already made *Un Chien andalou* and *L'Âge d'Or*, the latter 'a uniquely savage blend of visual poetry and social criticism,' according to writer Paul Hammond, a surreal masterpiece banned from public viewing thanks to Dalí's 'subversive eroticism' and the film's 'furious dissection of civilised values.'[1] Vicomte Charles de Noailles and his wife, Marie-Laurie, a descendant of the Marquis de Sade, had promised funds for the new film and Buñuel was anxious to have his writing partner on board.

But Dalí that summer had other manias in mind. He needed a muse and was pursuing the Russian beauty Gala, wife of poet Paul Éluard, and a significant, if controversial, figure in the surrealist movement. It was said that if one of the artists – Max Ernst, Yves Tanguy, Man Ray et al – did a particularly fine piece of work, the others would nod judiciously and whisper: 'Ah, but of course, he was having an affair with Gala at the time.'

Buñuel, with all the determination that was to characterize his career, followed Dalí from the shingle beach where fishermen repaired their nets, to the dining table where the local wine was said to have the bitter taste of tears, to the modest hut where his old student chum from Madrid's Residencia de Estudiantes had set up a studio. All to no avail.

In desperation, Buñuel tried to throttle Gala, to the consternation of the rest of the party: René Magritte, his dull wife, Georgette, art dealer Camille Goemans, and his svelte girlfriend, Yvonne Bernard. Cadaqués, despite its lack of a road, had been discovered by the Paris avant-garde and the appearance of this exotic group would be covered in the columns of the fortnightly *Sol Ixent*. Finally, his fingers prised from Gala's white throat, Buñuel packed his bag, shoved the script under his arm and sailed back around the coast, the still surface of the Mediterranean doing little to calm his fury. Salvador Dalí had worked on the scripts for two short films and Buñuel was now on his own.

He did not see Dalí again until 1937. Civil war had broken out in Spain. Fascist thugs had murdered their fellow student, the poet Federico García Lorca, and fearing that he was next on the list, Buñuel fled to New York, where Dalí, always one jump ahead, was safely ensconced with Madame Éluard. He was making a handsome living painting portraits of society ladies and collaborating on movie sets with Alfred Hitchcock.

Buñuel asked him for a $50 loan. But, just as Dalí had spurned working on short film number three, he refused his request and ended their long, fruitful friendship with a letter of such eccentric misanthropy, Buñuel's son, film-maker Juan Luis Buñuel (*Calanda*; *La Femme aux Bottes Rouges*), carries the offensive missive folded in his wallet to remind him of the joys of generosity.

Film-making is tough. Buñuel's flight from Spain at the outbreak of civil war, the banning of *L'Âge d'Or* and the long years of exile in Mexico were not wasted, but the very experiences that infused the wit and imagination that would make him one of the greatest film-makers of the twentieth century, as indeed, Salvador Dalí, who suffered his own array of paranoias and phobias, would become one of its great painters.

Buñuel's early films were random, scattered, indeed surreal, but he came to understand that the key to a great film is the script. If anything, the script for a short film is more important and perhaps more difficult to write than a feature, simply because the brush strokes by necessity must be fine and detailed, each moment perfect. He was learning his craft by trial and error and would have been the first to admit that he still had a long way to go. *Un Chien andalou* and *L'Âge d'Or* always head the Buñuel filmography, but he had already made with cameraman Albert Duverger back in 1929 the forgotten, five-minute short *Menjant garotes* (*Eating Sea Urchins*) on 35mm. Illustrating, perhaps, the incestuous nature of film-making, it was Salvador Dalí's young sister Ana María who had kept *Menjant garotes* stored in a biscuit tin where it remained until her death more than half a century later.

Shot for the most part in harsh sunlight, the film follows Dalí's plump father and stepmother as they stroll through the terraces of Cadaqués before sitting down to a plate of sea urchins. Buñuel had planned his set ups with care, the light filtering through the window as Dalí senior slices into his *garotes* revealing the first glimpse of a visual style that he would come to develop. But, a vital lesson to Buñuel, and all first-time film-makers, the film, for all the extravagance of camera angles and lighting effects and in spite of the Hannibal Lecter grin of Señor Dalí as he slurps down the first sea urchin, is so slender on story it is at best rather ordinary and, at worst, plain boring.

Buñuel needed Dalí's inspired if contradictory logic and had taken the train from Aragon in the hottest month of the year to try and get it. A phrase, a gesture, a jump-cut between unrelated events, a moment's silence or the introduction of music can make all the difference between success and failure, a story that grabs you and one that's as flat as the bay of Cadaqués in summer.

Film-making is a team process. Often, contacts made and films shared in the early days will last through a film-maker's career. Each film is a voyage of discovery and adventurers who have made the journey together before know they are with people they can rely on. Buñuel mastered his craft making short films and that is how most film-makers start. From Charlie Chaplin and Buster Keaton with their first silent movies to the current young auteurs Lynne Ramsey (*Ratcatcher*; *Morvern Callar*), Shane Meadows (*TwentyFourSeven*; *Once Upon a Time in the Midlands*) and Christopher Nolan (*Memento*; *Insomnia*) before tackling a feature, they cut their teeth on the silver ring of shorts.

It was Luis Buñuel's passion to make films that made him a film-maker, but there is another lesson to be learned from his flurry of activity that summer in 1929. *Menjant garotes* had been financed by his family, but getting it in the can, even if it was to remain hidden for decades, gave Buñuel the experience and, in turn, the confidence to go out and source funds for future projects.

For anyone on the same path today, the journey has never been easier. Cameras are smaller, lighter, less expensive and easier to use.

A home PC and a basic program are sufficient to edit film. And for anyone who wants to take the process to its ultimate conclusion, digital light processing and liquid crystal display home cinema projectors from Toshiba, Epson and others can turn the living room into a movie house. Anyone can do it.

How do you stand out in the crowd? How do you bring your movie gems into the world? Or, more important, in front of those who can make a difference to a new film-maker's career? The aim of this book is to begin to answer those questions and to inspire film-makers through the stages of writing, producing, financing, casting, directing, editing and exhibiting short films.

The book includes an analysis of the scripts of four very different shorts, a modern surrealist film, a horror tale, a comedy with Nick Moran as a fighter pilot and a *noir* thriller adapted from a short story.

In Buñuel's era, revolutionary politics or a flash of thigh was enough to make a film controversial. In an age when almost nothing is controversial, films will need other qualities.

L'Âge d'Or would remain banned for many years, but has since been shown on television and can be viewed at the surrealist galleries at the Tate Modern. When it was first screened in Britain, in Cambridge, in 1950, the sole complaint was from the RSPCA. Bare breasts and a nun being thrown from a window caused no offence, but one of the characters is seen booting a small dog up the backside. Social mores had changed, but not the English.

Note

1. Paul Hammond, *L'Âge d'Or* (BFI Publishing 1997)

Chapter 1

The Script

>> **H**OW DO YOU WRITE a short film?
There is a certain irony in the question in as much as the secret of writing a short film is the same as that of writing anything: the secret is there is no secret. It's plain hard work. Scriptwriting is rewriting. Whatever goes down on paper, however well it looks, and with the abundance of scriptwriting programs, it's probably going to look super, that first gush of words is unlikely to produce anything of great value. What that gush will do is give you something to work with. It is the cloth from which the tailor fashions a suit; the fittings are the rewrites, the new drafts.

It is often said that you should write about what you know about. I would amend that to say, better still, write about what moves you, your passions, dreams and desires. You have to get into the midst of the story before even you, the writer, knows what it is you are trying to say. Character drives plot, but the underlying theme, the message, is what holds the narrative together.

Once you give birth to your characters, they are responsible for their own actions, and the effects caused by those actions. Put a volatile character in a compromising situation and he will swing out with both fists; neither he nor you will be able to prevent it. Put temptation in the way of a thief and just watch his eyes light up as he looks for the main chance. Are we, the reader or viewer, interested in these people? Do we want to follow their story? Do the characters start at point A and shift subtly, cleverly, gradually and convincingly to point B? Will the brute learn self-control; the thief not to take what isn't given? Most important: is there conflict? All stories progress through conflict: action and reaction.

Boy asks Girl: Will you go to the movies with me? Girl says: Yes. No conflict, no story. Boy asks Girl: Will you go to the movies with me? Girl says: No. I can't stand men with beards.

Now we have a story. Will he shave off his beard for her? Will he shave it off in order to get her to see the movie with him, then grow it again once they're an item? And if he does regrow his beard, will she break off the relationship?

Now, we have conflict, the grist of every TV soap, but what underpins the story is the theme: the writer's viewpoint, the attitudes and issues the writer wants to explore. A theme can normally be expressed by a well-known saying, in this case: You can't tell a book by looking at the cover. In *The Wizard of Oz*, Dorothy discovers there's no place like home. *Rocky* learns if at first you don't succeed, you try, try, try again.

The Boy with the Beard is about superficiality, the comical aspects integral to the plot adding light relief, and underpinning the theme. When the Boy sees that the Girl is merely frivolous, he will stop pursuing her. The Girl, oblivious to her own nature, rather than looking in at herself, will look outward and seek ways of punishing the Boy. The initial point of conflict is the beard. The first turning point is when the Boy shaves off his beard to get a date. The plot requires another turning point, the second hook, to swing the story into a new direction.

In this case, we will add the Rival, the key element to most love stories and the third spar in the eternal triangle. Our Rival is a clean-shaven shallow character with an equal fondness for taking girls to the movies. When the Girl goes out with the Rival, she finds him self-centered, conceited, his conversation dull. She still hates beards, but will now look inside herself and realize that she has been superficial worrying over such trivialities. She has started to look inside the book, not just at the cover, and, as if she is looking in the mirror, she will glimpse in the reflection the danger of losing the man she really loves.

It is the emotional journey that holds readers and grabs an audience. To begin with, the Boy was pursuing the Girl. Now, the turnaround is complete. She will start pursuing him, extending the theme and highlighting this aspect of human nature: the tendency to reject what we have and miss it the moment it's gone.

With the story dynamic in flux and the characters now familiar, the scenes should turn with greater urgency, racing us to a conclusion that should achieve two goals:

1. to be both what the audience expects
2. yet not exactly in the way they expect it

The audience wants to be surprised, not disappointed by the obvious.

Each scene should have its own beginning, middle and end, a minor conflict leading to resolution and on to the next scene, the characters growing from each development. The effect is like placing tiles on a mosaic path, each contributing to the story's journey and driving us forward to a satisfying conclusion. If the story has been well told, the characters will have gone through changes. We will have observed their small imperfections, foibles and flaws, the acts of kindness and humanity that add up to the sum total of what they are, a representation of ourselves.

The metaphor of the sculptor releasing the figure from the block of marble is familiar and can be extended to the part played by the writer, the unique mannerisms, word patterns, strengths and weaknesses of his characters[1] laid bare as each new challenge chips away the outer layers to reveal the individual beneath. Our own dreams and deepest desires often remain a mystery to us; we are a collage of inconsistencies. But the writer must know his characters and their motivations; they must remain consistent *even as they change* in order for them to become interesting to the audience.

The Girl of our story will have fallen in love with the Boy for what he is, not how he appears, and will accept his facial hair. The Boy, conscious of her love and aware of the compromises she has made, will stop being so obstinate about his beard and perhaps shave it off for their wedding day, when the priest – this now being a Greek Orthodox story – has the longest beard known to humankind. The Rival, too, will have changed. He lost the girl, but has learned that you can't tell a book by looking at the cover.

The Boy with the Beard is a morality play that evolved *while I was writing it*. It began as a romantic comedy, but the weighty undertones could with careful writing and rewriting draw us into new depths: perhaps the Boy is a recent immigrant and wears the beard for religious reasons? Perhaps the Girl was once assaulted by a bearded man carrying a knife and the memory still haunts her?

If we take the cross-cultural theme, I would now name my characters: let's give the Boy the heroic-sounding name Alexander, the Girl Wendy, something fresh and easy on the tongue. The Rival we'll call Dirk, for reasons that will become clear. Writers keep books with titles like *Naming Your Baby* on their shelves and pay as much attention when christening their characters as parents give to naming their new-born infants. In Spain, people remember Don Quixote more than Cervantes, his creator. Great names of fiction live forever in our minds, Scarlett O'Hara, Sam Spade, Luke Skywalker, Lolita, Robin Hood, Nurse Ratched, Scrooge, Bond – James Bond. In *Pat Garrett and Billy the Kid* the chameleon-like Bob Dylan is named Alias.

The film *In the Heat of the Night* turns on the scene when gum-chewing police chief Rod Steiger asks Sidney Poitier his name.

'So, boy, what do they call you up there in the north?'

'They call me Mr Tibbs.'

The response earns Poitier respect and he states his name with such power the producers used the line to title the sequel. Good line, bad script. In the original, Poitier is picked up on a murder rap for no other reason than he's black. His knowledge, detective skills and humanity move the plot along and secure his release, but as a gritty look at Southern racism, the film is not about Poitier, but Steiger, as he comes to terms with his bigotry, his lack of humanity and, for good measure, his personal loneliness.

They Call Me Mr Tibbs is about *what it's about*, without sub-plots or theme; it lacks authenticity, the quality the writer should be striving for. If a scene doesn't work, only by looking for the veracity of the scene, for the authenticity of the characters' needs, desires and actions, will we unearth its weaknesses.

When a scene is stuck in as a device to move the plot along - 'Hi John, fancy seeing you here. Are you going to Anne's party at the country club Saturday?' – the filmgoer knows he's being made a fool of. It's a subtle thing like an instrument out of tune in an orchestra, but you can sense it in the auditorium when, instead of watching the screen, people are glancing around or – the ultimate nightmare – talking. You still see the above 'Hi John' scene, or the girlfriend opening a drawer by 'chance' and finding a gun hidden among the handkerchiefs, but this is lazy writing and it's growing harder to get away with it.

In this chapter and throughout the text, examples have been taken from features, not short films, simply because there are so few universally recognized short films to quote from. Writers of short films are presented with special difficulties, the challenge of space and time, or the lack of it. Once they overcome them, they will be ready to write a feature.

Going back to Wendy, if we want to run with the idea that she was assaulted, we could remap the story as gothic horror, a now clean-shaven Alexander becoming an avenging hero who pursues the bearded attacker to a haunted house on a windy cliff top where the rivals fight to the death. And who is the bearded attacker? Dirk, of course, in another guise, so named for the knife he carries.

When I was looking for a story to make the above example, a number of films rushed into my mind. But I needed something less complex, a fable, more than a feature. I was sitting with my morning coffee flicking through the local paper, avoiding the computer hum in the office next door. Writing is hard; it's always hard, any diversion to avoid it will do. I turned finally to the newspaper's back page and there was an attractive woman and a young man with a full beard pictured at their wedding; in their optimistic expressions was *The Boy with the Beard*, waiting to be found.

According to American writer and scholar Joseph Campbell, the stories are already there, inside us, bursting to come out.

> Whether we listen with aloof amusement to the dreamlike mumbo jumbo of some red-eyed witch doctor of the Congo, or read with cultivated rapture thin translations from the sonnets of the mystic Lao-tsu; now and again crack the hard nutshell of an argument of Aquinas, or catch suddenly the shining meaning of a bizarre Eskimo fairy tale: it will be always the one, shape-shifting yet marvellously constant story that we find, together with a challengingly persistent suggestion of more remaining to be experienced than will ever be known or told.[2]

The above paragraph comes from *The Hero with a Thousand Faces*, Campbell's analysis of world folk tales that shows how common threads and themes in storytelling bridge the frontiers of culture, religion and time. It was Campbell's study that inspired Christopher Vogler's *The Writer's Journey*, an insider's look at how writers can utilize mythic structures to create powerful narratives that are dramatic, entertaining and psychologically authentic. Since its first publication in 1998, *The Writer's Journey* has become the Hollywood 'bible' on the screenwriting craft.

The stories are there aplenty, in the depths of our own subconscious, and I quote Campbell to counter the postmodern belief that everything under the sun has already been seen and every story has already been told. In writing classes and spats among movie addicts someone will invariably remark that there is only a handful of different stories – the exact number varies – and writers throughout time just keep retelling them: *The Boy with the Beard* is *Romeo and Juliet*; the man with the fatal flaw – *Achilles*; the precious gift taken away – *Orpheus*; virtue finally recognized – *Cinderella*; a deal with the devil – *Faust*; the spider trapping the fly – Circe; change or transformation – *Metamorphosis*; the quest – *Don Quixote*.

To the list we can add the coming-of-age plot (*Gregory's Girl, On the Waterfront*); rivals (*Chicago, Amadeus*); escape (*The Great Escape, The Shawshank Redemption*); revenge (*Hamlet, Gladiator*); manipulation (*Svengali*). These stories have been reshaped over and over again, but it is the reshaping and combination of plots that make them fresh and original. Cross *Romeo and Juliet* with *Cinderella* and what do we end up with: the Richard Gere/Julie Roberts film *Pretty Woman*; change *Cinderella* for *Orpheus* and we have Nabokov's *Lolita*. The genius of George Lucas is that he borrowed from them all to create *Star Wars*, a mythical adventure in the tradition of *Gilgamesh*, the pre-Biblical epic still on the bookshelves today.

We are still discovering species of bird, insect and fish unknown to humankind. Every generation has its own hopes and fears, its own tales to tell: melting ice caps, vanishing rain forests, GM crops, terrorism. What makes our story special, what draws in the reader or viewer, then, is not the underlying mechanics of plot, but the characters. Great characters move the audience and, as plot unfolds through conflict, great villains make great stories.

Once born, before a word of narrative goes down on paper, writers should sketch out complete biographies of their characters, their ages, idiosyncrasies, disappointments, hopes and dreams, not caricatures or stereotypes, but flesh and blood originals with all the qualities, doubts and nervous tics that make us all one-offs. Characters need a past, a network of relationships. They show just a fraction of this, the tip of the iceberg, and then usually at a time of crisis. But from this study, you should be able to extract the essence of your characters and summarise them in a few sentences. Callie Khouri does it marvellously in her screenplay *Thelma and Louise*, describing Thelma's husband (the perfectly named carpet salesman Darryl) in three swift brushstrokes:

> Darryl comes trotting down the stairs. Polyester was made for this man and he's dripping in men's jewelry. He manages a Carpeteria.
>
> Darryl is checking himself out in the hall mirror and it's obvious he likes what he sees.
>
> He exudes overconfidence for reasons that never become apparent. He likes to think of himself as a real lady killer. He is making imperceptible adjustments to his over moussed hair. Thelma watches approvingly.[3]

What Callie Khouri did was take the traditional buddy movie and put two women in the lead roles. In the story, while Thelma is finding herself (coming-of-age), Louise is fighting the demons from the past. When they have fully matured into new beings, they know they can never go back to what they were; they are ready for the ultimate metamorphosis: the drive over the cliff edge into the Grand Canyon.

If the characters we create have a tale worth telling, they will *want* something: to escape to Mexico, get the girl, rob the bank, be a star, find El Dorado. A story becomes interesting when the writer sets up obstacles that prevent their heroes getting what they want (Thelma and Louise first lose their money, essential for their flight). The story hooks us as they overcome those obstacles and/or villains and thereby grow and change in the process. As the characters go through a range of emotions – fear, self-doubt, sorrow, elation – the audience will be seeing themselves in the hero or heroine and will be sharing those emotions. If you laugh out loud while reading a book or feel a tear jerk into your eye while you are watching a movie, the writer has done his job.

Thelma and Louise is often quoted on film courses and Callie Khouri's script should be on the reading list of every writer who wants to turn their pen to film, shorts or a feature, not only for its pace and dialogue, but for the symbolism neatly woven into the plot. *Thelma and Louise* is about male dominance, Darryl's comic machismo, the attempted rape and the truck driver's lecherous behavior subliminally underpinning that theme. Male domination is an abstract concept, but Callie Khouri has written scenes as symbols of that concept to make the abstract real and more easy to understand.

On the list of memorable names above is Nurse Ratched (Louise Fletcher) from *One Flew Over the Cuckoo's Nest*. The perfect use of symbolism is explored in this movie through the use of the water fountain McMurphy (Jack Nicholson) failed to budge on the various occasions when he tries to lift it. McMurphy is a free spirit gradually crushed by the institution. In the final scene, Big Chief (William Sampson) seizes the fountain and crashes it through the bars – to escape from the despotic asylum.

As a sub-plot, Big Chief's strand of the story tells us more about McMurphy, Nurse Ratched and oppression, underlining the theme. Sub-plots contribute color, comedy and nuance; they serve to confirm the main plot, reveal the contradictions of the principal characters and place obstacles in the hero's path. Characters who serve this function need as much fleshing out and, ideally, will go through changes during the course of events from one state to another, in the case of Big Chief, from tyranny to freedom.

One Flew Over the Cuckoo's Nest holds our attention because of the power of the characters drawn in Ken Kesey's novel. We as people are interested in the joys and suffering, the ups and downs of other people; at heart everyone is a gossip. Disney cartoons and science fiction monsters are anthropomorphic, and it will take rare skill for a writer to keep us involved in a plot where the hero goes into battle against some anonymous adversary like nature, disease, the tobacco companies or big business. The enemy needs a human face – Christopher Eccleston in Danny Boyle's virus nightmare *28 Days Later*; Michael Douglas as Gordon Gekko in *Wall Street*.

In life, the whistle-blower usually loses his battle against the corporate giants. It is the role of the writer to put the world back in balance and show us the little guy fighting back; except in downbeat *noir* and ironic tales, people come away from films more satisfied with positive endings. As Oscar Wilde reminds us: The good ended happily, the bad unhappily – that is fiction. Whether it's James Bond entering Ernst Blofeld's fortress, Rocky Balboa in the boxing ring, or Charlie Sheen challenging Michael Douglas in *Wall Street*'s final reel, the hero and the antagonist must have this conclusive, face-to-face confrontation to send the audiences home contented. The little guy rising to the challenge and overcoming evil appeals to our deepest humanity. We are the little guy.

One thing that first-time writers and film-makers need to overcome is that everyone has grown up on the same diet of countless movies and endless hours of television. We know how it's done because we've seen it done, over and over again. It looks easy. Film courses and text books, including this one, light the road before us. The struggle then, as Luis Buñuel understood, is to break the mould of our education and environment, think in fresh ways and use new technology to find our own originality.

Writing has laws of perspective, of light and shade, just as painting does, or music. If you are born knowing them, fine. If not, learn them. Then rearrange the rules to suit yourself.

What Truman Capote is saying in the above is that storytelling has rules, but like the navigator at sea with the moon and stars, we must still pilot our own course through the darkness.

Imagine a journey by land from London to Athens. We may take the ferry to Bilbao in Spain, cross the Pyrenees and hug the Mediterranean coast. Alternatively, we can take the tunnel to France, slip through Germany and Austria, then follow the Adriatic. The two journeys will be touched by different languages, foods, customs and landscapes; different people with different skills and knowledge will cross our paths along the way. But the destination is the same and the journey will be the hero's own personal and unique experience, the material face of the more profound internal journey.

All stories, long or short, for film or the written word, benefit from structure. In *The Writer's Journey*, cited above, Christopher Vogler outlines the twelve-stage journey the hero normally takes in those stories we find ultimately satisfying. A short film will lack time for all the intricate stages and archetypes, but a sense of structure is still crucial.

The eight-point guide below remains true to Vogler's principle, but is more practicable for a short film. I have applied the framework to both the short story and short film script in Chapter 9: *Greta May – The Adaptation*, and a careful reading reveals the eight steps that hold the story in place. The eight-point guide is not a formula, but a road map, and the best stories will take the framework and bend it into a new shape.

Making Short Films Eight-Point Guide

1. Introduce main character(s); set the scene.
2. Give the character a problem, obstacle, obsession or addiction.
3. Let the character work out a plan to overcome the problem.
4. Before setting out to solve the problem, there may be a moment of doubt that will require the hero to seek advice from a mentor: teacher, best friend. This is an opportunity to let the audience know more about the problem and weigh it up in their own minds. What would they do?
5. With new resolve (and often a *magical* gift from the mentor: the watches Q gives James Bond; Dorothy's ruby slippers), the hero sets out to overcome the problem, obstacle, obsession or addiction.
6. Overcoming the problem or challenge (getting the girl; escaping tyranny; saving the world) will be met by extreme opposition from the rival, who will usually have greater but different strengths and will in some ways bear similarities to the hero: the nemesis is the hero's dark side.

7. The hero will appear to fail in his quest. He will glimpse defeat, even death, and will require superhuman effort to overcome this daunting final task.

8. The hero wins the final battle, with an opponent, or enemy, or with himself, and returns to his natural state wiser, or stronger, or cured, but not necessarily happier. The journey has made him a different person. He has glimpsed death and can never go back to the simplicity of what he once was.

To the eight-point guide above, I would add the following recommendations when tackling a script.

Ten Tips

- Don't trust in inspiration, unless you want to be a poet. The first idea you get is often borrowed from every movie you've seen and book you've read.

- If you do work on that inspired project: rewrite, rewrite; rewrite. Those are the most important three things you will ever learn about scriptwriting, and I repeat: *rewrite, rewrite, rewrite.*

- See your writing from the other side of the screen, from the audience point of view; if there is no audience, there is no message.

- Do not adjust your writing to the market by attempting to stay abreast, or even ahead of changing trends; such work is a form of cultural static lacking veracity and, often, even relevance.

- Be true to your own vision. Write about what you know about? Absolutely. But then write what you believe in.

- Four steps to writing a short film scenario: find the ending; then the beginning; then the first turning point – the event

> that gets the story going; then the second turning point, the
> scene that swings the story around and sets up the ending.
> - Enter your story a short time before the crisis that ignites the
>   drama.
> - Scenes are like parties: arrive late and leave early.
> - Persevere.
> - Listen to criticism. But don't always take it.

I repeat the first line of this chapter: How do you write a short film?
It requires the same intense work as writing a feature or novel, it's
just shorter. Finally, a quote from Jean Cocteau:

> Listen carefully to first criticisms of your work. Note just what
> it is about your work the critics don't like – then cultivate it.
> That's the part of your work that's individual and worth keeping.[5]

Poet, dramatist, novelist, film director, the kind of guy you could really
grow to hate, Cocteau began his career with *The Life of a Poet*, a short
film.

Notes

1. Throughout the text, I use masculine nouns and pronouns to refer to
   both sexes; while this avoids clumsy tags like cameraman/woman or
   soundperson, it should also be made clear that there are now just as many
   female producers in the industry as males, as indeed there are many
   female directors, editors etc.
2. Joseph Campbell, *The Hero with a Thousand Faces* (Fontana Press,
   1993)
3. Callie Khouri, *Thelma and Louise*
4. Truman Capote
5. Jean Cocteau

Chapter 2

The Producer

>> **W**HEN A NOVELIST COMPLETES a manuscript, apart from the rewrites and brawls with the editor, the job is done. With a screenplay, the journey is about to begin.

With short films, the writer, director and producer will often be one and the same. Film-makers, though, will mostly find that life is too short to keep so many balls in the air all at once and, when they find what they are best at, they stick to it.

The foundation of every film, as the previous chapter makes clear, is the script, but it is the producer who will nurture the writer through the new drafts, fork out for the cappuccinos, then present the final version to the director, casting agent, actors and funders. He will draw up contracts, speak to lawyers, settle feuds and stroke the high-strung sensitivities of his family of creatives.

In the 2002 *Simone*, Winona Ryder is furious with Al Pacino because her trailer, while the biggest on the lot, isn't actually the highest. At first Pacino tries to let the air out of the tyres on the offending vehicle, but when his patience runs out, he does the only self-respecting thing left to him and fires her. In this parody on the movie business, Miss Ryder, in a refreshing self-parody, is replaced with a computer generated star character. Such technology isn't yet with us, but the scene illustrates perfectly the relationship between the producer and his team, his role as best friend, adviser, marriage counsellor, guru, psychiatrist and, ultimately, the boss. From the moment a film goes into production, whether it's a Hollywood feature or a first short, the meter is running and the producer has to keep his eyes on the clock.

It is often assumed outside the industry that the producer has a fat wallet from which he pulls fists full of dollars like Michael Lerner as the odious Jack Lipnick in *Barton Fink*. Not in real life. Tim Bevan and Eric Fellner at Working Title are responsible for a string of hits, *Four Weddings and a Funeral*, *Notting Hill*, *Bridget Jones's Diary*,

Love. . . Actually, but are backed by American studios. The producer uses other people's money and only when he hands that money back with a slice of the profits will he raise funds for the next project.

There is another common misconception to bear in mind: even a no-budget film is going to cost somebody something somewhere along the line: the camera and equipment, postage, labels, pre-production planning, post-production film developing or transfer, and that's apart from the bus fares and bacon sandwiches during production. The producer with his pared down micro-budget short may not have investors to worry about, but will need to show flair with his debut in order to attract some cash next time around.

It's not essential for the producer to have a sister working in Barclays in Soho or a college buddy at the Chase Manhattan; what he does need is a nose for a story and the passion to convince backers and funders (more on that later) to finance his project over the many competing and perhaps equally good packages that flood across their desks. You will notice that, in the mind of the producer, the script has become the product and the product, with its added elements, becomes a package.

The producer, then, is a salesman, a PR shape-shifter; he can sell plans for a bridge when there isn't a river; he is a UN peacekeeper between warring factions – the writer, director, leading lady – a shepherd who should guide his creatives and, as such, is a creative himself. You don't have to be able to score music to appreciate Mozart or Ry Cooder's seductive blues. Likewise you don't need to know what the *f* stops do on a camera, or how an editor adds fades on an Avid Composer. What the producer understands is human nature. He knows how to get the best out of his people and gives the best in return.

Producers are characterized as tough guys, the cigar-chomping tight wad. While this might be true of a Hollywood Jack Lipnick, the parody is the exception and, in my own encounters with industry heavyweights, I have experienced only kindness and that species of vibrant, boundless energy it takes to be interested in everything and everyone they come across – the energy it requires to make movies.

One time, when I was writing a book about Salvador Dalí, I met Hal Landers, the man behind such classics as *What ever Happened to Baby Jane?* I mentioned that I was a writer – writers can't help themselves – and Hal asked to read the manuscript. It was something I would not normally have done, showing someone unfinished work, but I was swept along by Hal's enthusiasm. The following morning, he insisted on calling a publisher he knew. That same day, the publisher was calling me and by the end of the week I was reading a contract. There was nothing in this for Hal Landers – except the dedication on the flyleaf – but he had used his contacts to pull the deal together, extended his own network and made life seem truly magical.

Hal Landers once bumped into Queen Juliana of Holland in a store in Paris. 'Hey,' he said, 'aren't you the Queen of Holland? I'm from New Jersey; I've never met a queen before. Why don't you let me buy you a cup of coffee?' The Queen was so overwhelmed by the approach she agreed, and they remained friends from that day on.

What these anecdotes illustrate is that the qualities Hal Landers brought to his daily life are the very qualities required by a producer: enthusiasm, energy, generosity, a good eye for product (the Dalí book is now in its fifth edition), an agile mind, the verve to think laterally and the personality to do the unusual. Like invite queens for coffee.

One time when I was in Paris, I was invited to the premier of *The Rainbow Thief*, a whimsical fantasy written by Berta Dominguez D., directed by Alexandro Jodorowsky and pairing Peter O'Toole with Omar Sharif for the first time since *Lawrence of Arabia*. I met the producer, Alexander Salkind, and at his prompting I told him that I was trying to interest broadcasters in a documentary project. He didn't make any phone calls on my behalf, but led me to the bar and told me how he got started in the film business.

He had arrived penniless in France from Russia and was taking a train from Paris to Lyon where he thought he might have more luck finding work. In the carriage, he met a man who owned three shoe shops. Alex told him a story he wanted to turn into a short film. By the time they arrived at their destination, the shoe shop owner was so intrigued, he decided to sell one of his shops and fund the movie. Financially, it was a disaster. Salkind was depressed, but it was his first film and his collaborator, the shoe shop guy, considered the experience so valuable, he sold a second shop to finance the next film. That, too, was a flop, but he had started out on a course from which he saw no way back: he sold the last of his shops to fund one more film and lost everything.

Alex Salkind had to go elsewhere for finance, but he now had a showreel and was on his way. As for the shoe shop proprietor, he'd left the footwear business behind him forever. He'd caught the film bug, worked as Salkind's assistant and had a long career as a cinematographer. Salkind had learnt was the three essential lessons:

1. How to inspire potential finance.
2. How to manage a budget.
3. How to tell a good story.

With these skills he went on to make an enormous variety of movies, from Kafka's impenetrable *The Trial* (1962) to *The Three Musketeers* (1973) to the *Superman* movies where, due to deft negotiations and deceptive scheduling, his name was lent to what lawyers call the Salkind Clause: that an actor must be told *how many movies he's making.* When he filmed Christopher Reeve in the first *Superman* in 1977, the out-takes contained much of the footage used in *Superman II.*

Salkind by then was a powerful figure, 'a Russian producer who moves somewhat mysteriously in international circles,[1] according to writer John Walker, but he had learned when he was penniless the value of a penny and never took his eye off the ticking meter. The producer will always be pushing the production manager and first assistant director (first AD) to keep to schedule, that's his job. But the enthusiasm and passion he brings to the project must animate them to give their best. He will develop the bilingual skill of telling his director two things at once: The rushes are great. Get on with it. He will know when his leading lady needs complimenting or firing. Producing is a multi-skilled pursuit and communication skills form the basis of all the others.

The bigger the budget, the more of other people's money he's spending and the good producer will always be aware of that responsibility. He makes a modest living from the fee written into the budget. He makes the big money for those fat cigars from the points, the percentage of profits negotiated with finance or the studios. The success of a film will leverage up those points for future projects. Failure will make it that much more difficult to finance the next one and sobering statistics from the Film Council show that the majority of first-time film-makers never make a second feature.

To turn the written word into film needs everyone from the stars whose names go up in lights to the lowliest runner on a work experience scheme. The process of mixing and shaping the many disparate elements is like taking base metal and turning it into gold. The producer is the alchemist. Behind the scenes he will be working harder than anyone. It's his reputation that's on the line.

A variety of prefixes shore up the title producer: Assistant, Associate, Executive, Line and the modest Co. However, what we are dealing with here is *the* producer, the man or woman who finds the raw material: the book, play, short story, original script, a script adapted from another medium, an idea on the back of a pack of cigarettes, or inspired by a photograph on somebody's shelf – and what he sees is the film flashing before his eyes.

This talent is more acquired than innate and, for the producer to get started, the short film provides the same demands of story-telling and film-making found in a feature or TV drama. The constraints of budget and the need to answer to backers or broadcasters will encourage the producer to seek out a story that works for a wide audience, and that's not a bad thing. However, if you do have the urge to make something culturally or socially valid, a personal crusade, a showcase for your six-year-old twins, or something zany and completely off-the-wall like Martin Pickles' *G.M.*, a short homage to Georges Méliès (discussed in Chapter 7), the short film has all the challenges of a feature without the risks, critically as well as financially.

The first job is to find the script or find the story and put a writer to work on it. Where do you find a writer? Throw a stone out of the window and you'll probably hit one. Finding a good writer – finding a great writer, that takes time, practice, patience – and luck.

If you announce that you're looking for material, proposals will start dropping through the mail box with whining letters that diligently explain the story, always the kiss of death; if a script needs explaining, it isn't ready. Andrea Calderwood once remarked that, when she left BBC Scotland for Pathé, the same scripts followed her down the M6 to London. She took on two assistants, they read 700 scripts between them and rejected the lot. That isn't to say, of course, that the 701st isn't going to be *the one*!

It's an odd contradiction, but even with all those rookie writers out there, producers from the narrow streets of Soho to the gleaming glass offices looming over Santa Monica Boulevard are pulling their hair out weeping over the scarcity of good scripts. There was a time when every man leaning on every bar imagined he had a book in him. Now it's a screenplay. In fact, mention the movie business, and he'll whip it out of his shoulder bag, dog-eared and coffee-ringed, and ask strangers casually met if they would like to take a look. If you meet Andrea Calderwood in the bar she'll probably tell you she's a dentist.

While there are thousands of people writing scripts, producers continue to complain that there isn't anything worth filming, and with the complaint being ubiquitous, there must be something to it. Producers are therefore rejecting the scripts sliding over the transom and are making calls to publishing houses in search of the neglected novel, the remaindered gem, the book out of copyright. Others are venturing out of the West End to see fringe plays, and into the wind blown canyons off-Broadway to hole-in-the-wall experimental theaters. If it's worth publishing or staging, it must be worth taking a look at.

But here lies the dilemma. The novel is about ideas, about the internal life of the characters. Proust in *Remembrances of Things Past* wanders off for a dozen pages to describe the smell of *madeleines*. Try getting your writer to put that in his screenplay. Or try getting him to take it out if he's attempted to slip it in. The stage play is about words, plays on words, the taste of words. There is a mass of material that can be adapted, but as anyone who has ever done any adapting soon learns, you have to read the original, take out the kernel and sling the rest to the pigeons. An adaptation is just as hard to write as an original screenplay, perhaps harder.

A friend of mine recently quit making corporate videos to adapt a biography, the hardest of genres. Within days he was phoning to chat about migraine and insomnia; his attraction to cliff tops and razor blades. Suddenly he was fighting with his girlfriend – her fault – and arriving late for appointments; he was drinking too much or, alternatively, claiming he no longer drank at all (first sign of the alcoholic). Finally, he turned up at a meeting wearing odd shoes. He talked about the 'verbal' power of silent movies then handed me a Post-it with this on it:

> The true way leads along a tight-rope, which is not stretched aloft but just above the ground. It seems designed more to trip than to be walked along.

He'd found Franz Kafka, or Franz Kafka had found him, and this is where the producer becomes the psychiatrist, the healer, the script editor. My writer friend was filled with self-doubt, not that he had done a bad job with the screenplay, he just needed someone to tell him he'd done a good job, a great job. . . just a few tweaks here and there, get the first turning point forward a few pages, put some action into that soggy middle. . . maybe cut out that section on page 73 where the cop explains the whys and wherefores to his sergeant.

Producer Maureen Murray (*The Sea Change*) puts smiley faces beside the bits she likes in a script and her writers are more able to cope with the cold straight lines that slice like razors through the bits she doesn't. She makes suggestions, but expects the writer to find solutions: the two skills are different and must compliment each other like *yin* and *yang* in a perfect if reversed fit.

A producer is not a writer who has too much in the in tray to write, but must be able to distinguish good writing when it's on the page and bad writing that needs erasing. Rewrites are a form of torture, 'the main condition of the artistic experience,'[2] according to Samuel Beckett, but no screenplay surfaces through the slush piles without them. A film may not live up to the script's potential, but there has never been a great film made from a bad script.

Some writers are good at dialogue, others structure, others still can see the big picture and take on adaptations. There are writers like Paul Schrader – *Taxi Driver*, *Cat People* – who go alone into the desert for a week, work twenty hours a day and return with a finished scenario. Maybe it needs fixing, but there's another kind of writer unique to the film industry, the script doctor, and that's what he does, not original work but, like a picture restorer, he fills in the fine details.

The role of the producer is to match the writer with the story; in Hollywood, of course, they'll use a combination of expertise and leave the Writer's Guild to resolve the credits.

There is yet another kind of writer the producer must watch out for and he's the one who does a single draft and is reluctant to do more because he knows the script will be overhauled when a director comes on board. He's right, of course, it will be. But a director won't come on board if the script isn't fully developed in the first place. These writers, normally very competent, make a reasonable living writing first drafts and can't understand why it's rare for their scripts to turn into films. They are often wonderful raconteurs and can slip marquee names with their business cards into every conversation. These are the writers to avoid. Their stories are verbal, not on the page, and it is easy to be fooled by a colorful personality unless the producer has knowledge of script mechanics and the insight to enjoy their company and leave it at that.

If the producer has learned the art of managing money, he should max out his credit cards and spend some time on a desert island finding out how stories work. Read Æschylus, the lives of the great Olympians, Oedipus and on to Shakespeare and Chaucer. Dip into the wise worlds of Lao-tsu and Confucius; some Jacobean drama, and don't forget the exquisitely constructed short stories of Hemingway and James Joyce. See Sam Beckett's absurdist plays (demand them on your island) and study the greats: Dickens, Thomas Hardy, E.M. Forster, Daphne du Maurier, F. Scott Fitzgerald, Flaubert, William Golding. . . and on to Tolkein, Nick Hornby, J.K. Rowling. . . Gore Vidal and Michel Houellebecq.

You can learn a lot about making films by watching films, but you learn story-telling from the written word. Buñuel hitched his wagon on to Dalí's genius to get started, but he was a voracious reader and became a masterly writer with the breathtaking *Belle de Jour* and Academy Award winning *The Discreet Charm of the Bourgeoisie*, to name just two of his many films. To get there, like Buñuel, it makes sense to start with shorts. Once you get those right, you'll have a show-reel for Andrea Calderwood to brighten her quest for the perfect script.

Unlike those made in the United States and in Europe, many short films made in the UK have a sameness about them, no doubt because the majority are produced by young film-makers eager to enter the industry and whose background and education are similar. They have the mixed good fortune not to have lived through the hard times of Alexander Salkind, who fled Russia, or Hal Landers, who grew up in the mean streets of New Jersey during the Depression, though, naturally, it is those experiences that shaped them and gave them an edge, the nerve it takes to approach strangers on a train and royals out shopping.

According to Dawn Sharpless, creative director at Dazzle Films, one of the UK's top outfits for sales, distribution and the exhibition of short films, shorts in the UK are falling behind because insufficient time is spent on their development. Short films are often seen as merely a stepping stone to features and film-makers are in such a hurry to take that step they are not putting the time into creating powerful short scripts. The short film discipline is a genre in its own right, and only when that is fully recognized and appreciated will short films improve. 'Occasionally something makes you sit back in your seat and you realize that here's a film-maker with a story to tell,' Dawn adds.[3] 'But the sad thing is that for every fifty shorts I see, you sit back only once with real excitement.'

What's the problem?

'Inadequate planning. I think the whole secret is in pre-production,' she says. 'New film-makers need to be more daring. Stories should take us to places we have never been to before – and that takes courage.'

Her observation is substantiated by Elliot Grove, who heads the Raindance Film Festival. Some 2,000 shorts are submitted to him each year from forty or so countries, and 200 make it into the annual festival, the largest showcase of shorts in the UK. He has noticed that every year there is a flood of good shorts from a different country. Last year it was Poland; a few years ago, South Africa. 'It's always somewhere new, but it has been a few years since I have seen anything in the UK that really knocks your socks off.'

Elliot Grove has noticed that most British short films are dialogue driven, while those in the United States and Europe tend to be more visual. 'It's an odd dichotomy, because those British films that are visual usually go around the world winning prizes.'

In the US and Canada, young film-makers have grown up on a diet of MTV, while in the UK, a lot of scripts and films Grove sees have been inspired by TV soaps with their incessant banter and lack of action. With shorts, film-makers should be exploring ideas and learning their craft, says Grove. They should study as many short films as they can, especially at festivals, where they will come in contact with other film-makers meeting the same challenges and where they can ask each other how they got this effect or that shot. Film is a collaborative process, and Elliot Grove has been constantly and pleasantly surprised at how willing film-makers are when it comes to sharing information.

Grove compares the difference between writing a short film and a feature to the difference between creating a haiku poem and a sonnet. 'It requires different techniques, different skills, a different sensibility. With a good short film you have a calling card. And every time we have shown a film-maker with great story-telling skills, they have moved on to making successful features.'

Raindance first showed Christopher Nolan's shorts before he made *Following* and *Memento*, and showed Shane Meadows before he made *TwentyFourSeven*.

If in the search for a feature, producers look at novels and plays, for a short film, one surprisingly untapped source of material is the short story, sadly neglected by mainstream publishers and mainly found in the hermetic world of the literary magazine.

There are thousands of small press journals with a constant flow of new stories, usually by writers experimenting with style and who view publication as an end in itself. Few journals can afford to pay contributors, but the competition to get into print is still fierce and the quality of writing often very high. Short story writers know every word counts and, as a form, the short story has similarities to the short film that do not apply to the novel and play. Both make use of sugges-tion, atmosphere, nuance, the subtly implied gesture. Both are a riddle, every word having to carry its own weight, justify its existence. The short story weaves fine lines more than broad strokes. Explanation is death. A published story would have been honed and refined, every gesture thought through to such a degree that if the woman in the story runs her tongue over her lips, there is such a good reason for it, you'd better make sure your script contains the same instruction and your director heeds it.

Where do you find these literary and small press magazines? On the web. In the library. On the shelves in independent book shops. Find one, and you find them all. Research is money in the bank, the first weapon in the producer's armory. And if you do hit on a writer with a fine short story, he will already be well versed in rewriting and prepared for it when you option a short script. And who knows, perhaps he has a feature script lurking in the bowels of his laptop?

Short stories are subtle, often enigmatic, with carefully drawn characters, and when film-makers alight on them they tend to think in terms of features not shorts. There are many examples of successful adaptations, among the best known coming from three Philip K. Dick stories: Ridley Scott's *Bladerunner*, from the imaginatively titled *Do Androids Dream of Electric Sheep?* Steven Spielberg's *Minority Report*, and John Woo's 2003 adaptation of *Paycheck*, a story about a machine that can read the future and just as relevant in film terms half a century after it was first published in 1953. Dawn Sharpless was unable to come up with any examples of short stories that have been turned into memorable short films, but yearns for the day when that hole in the genre is filled.

Instead of doing their research and finding material, producers in frustration turn to directors and accept their scripts, not because they're better, often it's the contrary, but at least they know the director is committed and they haven't got to go through the birth pains of yet another draft. The result, though, as Dawn Sharpless has observed, are too many forgettable films - shorts and features - written by non-writers and backed by producers too uncertain of themselves to find a writer and put in the hours bonding and working together. Writers tend to be introvert. Directors are charming, outgoing, more fun to work with. But producers should be wary and heed William Goldman's haunting counsel: there are three essentials that come before you sign up a director. The Script. The Script. And the Script.

When Goldman's *Butch Cassidy and the Sundance Kid* came out, New York's three leading papers devoted many pages to their reviews. Two of the critics were in raptures over the Redford/Newman coupling and forgot to mention the writer. The third hated the picture and blamed the script. Goldman had spent five years sitting in his New York apartment writing it.

Critics are not going to go easy on writers. The producer must. He should cultivate the wisdom of ancient China where the Emperor once sent an emissary to Lao-tsu asking for advice on how to rule the kingdom. You should rule the kingdom, replied the sage, as you would cook a small fish.

Producers are emperors. Writers are small fish. Don't grill them, don't batter, bone and leave them gutted. Writers are delicate: fine porcelain; thin ice on winter morning ponds; a love affair. Imagine the plumber coming three days late to repair the loo. He shoves a new tube into the ballcock, fingerprints the tiles with lubricating oil and you feel a wave of gratitude when he accepts $300 cash and agrees to screw the government out of the taxes. Your writer drops in with three typos and an oxymoron fleshing out a secondary character and you want to kill him. Those stains on the bathroom walls have to be douched away and where better to spray some ammonia than at the self-doubting wordsmith. Writers cry easily. Don't use words like: pretentious, slow, lacking, boring, depressing or another day, as in: 'We'll talk about it another day.'

He'll worry himself sick waiting for that day. Let slip the word pretentious and you're leaving yourself open to the pretensions of defining the term. Tell a writer his script's slow and he'll shuffle down to Starbucks for a double espresso with whipped everything, including the skin on his back. Tell him his work's depressing and he'll get depressed, swallow a fistful of painkillers and consider Hemingway's last dance with a shotgun.

The major production companies work with established writers and, more than ever, are sourcing material from novels, biographies and plays. The new producer is more likely to be working with an inexperienced writer who, like the producer, is learning his craft. The writer will work for weeks and months before presenting what he believes is a masterpiece and it will require tact and patience for him to see that what he has typed is probably little more than a glorified treatment.

When Lee Hall's script for *Billy Elliot* first went to the BBC it was about the miners' strike in Thatcher's Britain. Billy's desire to dance was a sub-plot. Hall's standpoint was socialist more than aspirational. Three years of development changed a story about class solidarity to one about class betrayal, from Old Labour to New Labour, and created a film for our times. Hall's first draft, like all first drafts, was not a film but a road map leading to a film, a guide, not the place it became. When you read first drafts you are looking for a spark, originality, an individual voice, not gold dust but the iron ore that can be mined and shaped into a bridge to span the gulf from development to production. A producer should identify all that is good in a script. If only 10 per cent is good, salvage it, compliment it. Get rid of the 90 per cent and start again.

Billy Elliot spent three years in development. *Good Will Hunting* needed seven. Richard Attenborough was white haired and twenty years older before *Gandhi* was ready to go. Scripts are hard to write, as difficult or more difficult than novels. They need many drafts and time, lots of time. Producers must face that. They choose a companion as much as a project. Their writer becomes their brother, their sister, their child. According to Cyril Connolly, writers are just that, infants crying in their cots for attention. A writer needs faith, patience and passion. A producer needs all of that and a box of kleenex to wipe away the tears.

There is no science for putting producers and writers together, although an experiment to do just that has been created by two London-based organizations, the New Producers Alliance and Screenwriters' Workshop with their script initiative Match. Screenwriters armed with treatments are paired with first-time producers, recognized script editors are attached as godfathers and, with their input, projects are developed for their journey into the industry. Since the scheme started in 2001, Marcus Lloyd's script *Cuckoo* has won the prestigious £10,000 Oscar Moore Foundation Screenwriting Prize, and other projects have been optioned by major production companies.

When a producer finds his writer he sticks with him. *The Claim* (2000) was produced by Andrew Eaton with Frank Cottrell Boyce writing and by the time Michael Winterbottom began directing in Canada, they were already working on *24 Hour Party People*, the next project.

At a Script Factory screening of *The Claim*, Cottrell Boyce spoke about the long process he'd gone through to take the themes from Thomas Hardy's *The Mayor of Casterbridge* and transpose them to the 1849 gold rush in the American West. He told the audience the first drafts (that's plural) of his scripts are done *just to see what the themes are*. The next drafts have to be a good read so that the *Suits* with their check books can see the story in their minds. The script that goes out to actors is slightly different again. *But every draft is different to the shooting script.* Those earlier drafts contain an explanation of themselves that you don't need when you're ready to shoot. It's a leaner and fitter thing. 'I love this stage. It's really great when you feel something coming to life. It's like cutting diamonds.'

Frank Cottrell Boyce did not choose to write *The Claim*. Andrew Eaton chose it and stuck Hardy's novel on his desk. Of course, writers want to write their own stories. But it is the job of producers to know what they can market. With a short film, the producer has an added burden: telling a good story in ten minutes is hard and finding slots for films that are longer is harder still, as we shall discuss later when it comes to distribution.

Once the producer has survived the writing process and has a script in his hand, he moves to the next square on the board where he must find a director and build his team.

Notes

1. John Walker
2. Samuel Beckett
3. The quotations in this chapter from Dawn Sharpless and Elliot Grove are from interviews with the author.

Chapter 3

The Director

>> T HE WRITER HAS LABORED over his ten, descript-
ive, lively but tightly written pages, and the producer
hands this precious object to the director. It is hardly
surprising that writers want to direct their own work but this impulse
is, in an historic sense, a relatively new trend and many subscribe to
Hitchcock's faith in what he called The Trinity: Writer. Director.
Producer. By keeping the roles of writer and director separate, the
producer has greater control.

In the case of Hitchcock, while he was directing one film, every
morning he would have breakfast with the writer he'd set to work on
a new project. He didn't read the pages or interfere with the ongoing
narrative, but like the operator of a Punch and Judy show, his hand
was manipulating the twists and turns from behind the scenes.

The director, whatever his modus operandi, will invariably work
on the script and his name often finds its way on to the writing credits,
something Hitchcock grandly renounced. The director also gets the
debatable designation *A Film By . . .* just above or just below the title,
depending on his status and the power of his agent when it comes to
negotiating the contracts. The deifying of the director in this way
occurs because he is the creator of the finished work, the *auteur*, a
term introduced into film language in the 1960s by critics to describe
directors whom they considered had a discernible style or message
running through their work. The director is the artist who takes the
raw material of the script and combines the elements of mise en scène,
a phrase borrowed from the theatre and meaning 'to put on stage.'

In film terms, John Gibbs in his excellent study *Mise-en-Scène*
suggests a useful definition might be the contents of the frame and
the way those contents are organized, both halves of the formulation
being significant:

> What are the contents of the frame? They include lighting,
> costume, décor, properties, and the actors themselves. The

organisation of the contents of the frame encompasses the relationship of the actors to the camera, and thus the audience's view. So in talking about mise-en-scène, one is also talking about framing, camera movement, the particular lens employed and other photographic decisions. Mise-en-scène therefore encompasses both what the audience can see, and the way in which they are invited to see it. It refers to many of the major elements of communication in the cinema, and the combinations through which they operate expressively.[1]

In the novel, the word alone must convey mood and meaning. In film, every frame is packed with information, a shadow, a ticking clock, the breeze fingering the curtains: every detail is significant. Stephen Fry while directing *Bright Young Things* (2003) from the Evelyn Waugh novel *Vile Bodies* was shown by the props department several cigarette cases from the 1930s for him to choose from. The chosen cigarette case may only be seen for a fraction of a second – it may be edited out of the final cut – but it is the attention to detail that creates audience identification with characters and involvement in their lives.

The director must have an eye for every small detail. He decides who does what, when and why, this multiplicity of detail described by actor Gary Oldman after the first time on the floor as 'death by a thousand questions.'[2]

The fusion of these disparate parts is the puzzle the director (with the editor's help) assembles and it is his vision that we see on screen. Of all the jobs in film, the director's requires the least training and the least experience with technology. That isn't to say that directors do not know their way around an editing suite, or which filters to use on the camera. Most do. The best learn. What the director needs most, however, is the insight to understand immediately what the story is about, what passions drive the characters, and what each actor needs in order for them to make those passions real.

When we think back on any situation, in the pub with friends, a bitter row, a day on the beach, a night of love, we see it from our own point of view. As we piece the memory together, the mind selects the most salient and piquant details with camera angles, distances, juxtapositions, close-ups and long shots in a richly woven tapestry.

This selection of fragments is the same as taking frames of film and, in our heads, cutting movies from our recollections. According to anthropologists, once monkeys learn to use tools, to prise open sea shells, for example, future generations are genetically blessed with that knowledge. Likewise, a century after the Lumière Brothers first shot moving pictures, it seems an innate human predisposition to be able to piece together the puzzle of a film story and, perhaps more important, to actively take part in its telling by incorporating our own experience and imagination.

Actors develop and refine this art; the director like a hypnotist will draw out the appropriate memories to bring a scene to life. You don't have to be an out of work father with hungry mouths to feed to play the role, as Clint Eastwood showed in *Unforgiven*, the story of a retired gunslinger who crawls back into his old skin in order to put food on the table. Similarly, it's unlikely in Beverly Hills that Sigourney Weaver would have come face to face with an *Alien* bent on genocide (though anything's possible in Beverly Hills). Both performances were convincing because these proficient actors are able to dredge up emotions that inform their characters.

The director must know the character he is creating as well or *even* better than the actor; the evolution of their story will be part of the pattern painted inside his mind. Shooting schedules by necessity divide scripts into convenient but disconnected chunks that are stuck together when filming is completed. Cinema actors are trained to give realistic performances with minimal preparation; it is considered by many that too much preparation can blunt their edge, the reverse of work in theatre, where rehearsals are lengthy and stories are told chronologically.

A woman, for example, who stabs her husband and is taken away by *gendarmes* in a rainy Paris exterior, may not get to show what led up to the fatal event until weeks later when the crew moves to do the villa interiors in sun-drenched St Tropez. If the director dresses the woman in the Paris scene in a clinging gown that becomes diaphanous in the spring rain, it's going to look a whole lot different than if she's wearing an anorak and climbing boots. Are her shoulders sagging, or does she hold her head high? Is mascara running in black streams over her cheeks or are her scarlet lips puckered in a defiant smile? Was her husband a brute and were we with her, feeling her pain and relief as she plunged the knife in his back? Or is she a scheming gold digger who deserves the guillotine? How the audience reacts depends on the scene staged by the director and the performance drawn from the actress.

To return to *Unforgiven*, Clint Eastwood would not have approached the role by trying to *act* the feeling of a man suffering the torments of failure. Rather, he would have allowed the appropriate consciousness to take possession of him. That state would generate the emotionally applicable movements, responses, behavior and body language, a glimpse into the inner soul where all sensation occurs on a deeper level. It is the art of restraint and suggestion that Eastwood has mastered, a particular achievement as he normally directs himself.

More than the writer who has shaped his theme, plotted his turning points and set up his surprises, the director would have combed the material for the emotionally charged moments and, through his cast, reveals the heart of character. An actor well directed will make his feelings so clear that lines in the dialogue mentioning love, despair, jealousy, hatred and so on can be edited out of the final cut, the telling having been supplanted by showing, the point made by Frank Cottrell Boyce in the previous chapter, his diamond-cutting analogy for the shooting script being that moment when the last traces of dust are blown away and the sparkling gemstone is revealed.

A film goes through three stages to reach completion: pre-production, production and post-production. All carry equal weight and, as the producer will remind his director, it is in pre-production where they can save time and money on production and post. The ticking clock is the perfect symbol for the process: for the producer the ticking clock is a meter ringing up the bills; for the director, the ticking clock is more like a metronome guiding rhythm and pace; for the audience the ticking clock is a ticking bomb that holds us breathless waiting for the explosion. The director will keep us waiting, building the sense of urgency, the tension.

Typically, the writer would indicate in a script:

The Firefighter dashes like a 100 metre sprinter into the blazing building to save the baby.

But the Mother's reaction, the Fire Chief's reaction, the play of water arcing from the hoses, the size of the flames leaping from the building, to what degree the staircase inside is turning to ash; when exactly the Mother's reaction and the Fire Chief's reaction are inserted, and how many times they're inserted; the swelling crowd, the swirling police lights and the look on the Firefighter's blackened face as he scoops the infant into his arms: all this – along with set design, costume, the music score – are created by the director from the screenplay's brief scene description.

If the blaze is the first scene in a movie (and it's a powerful opening), how the Firefighter plays it, and how the director guides him, depend on how future events unfold. It certainly looks like this guy is our hero, the character we want to identify with, but it requires the whole story for us to understand his action, his motivations, whether he's a coward overcoming cowardice, an ego maniac playing to the crowd, a man whose wife has just died *in a fire* and who has nothing to live for. Perhaps the Fire Chief is his older brother, or *younger* brother. The fact that we don't know is what makes the scene interesting. Conversely, the director may give the audience superior position, whereby we in the darkened auditorium know something the Firefighter doesn't – *perhaps it is his baby in the cot?* – and we watch with vicarious angst as this is revealed.

Don Roos's 1998 *The Opposite of Sex* opens with Christina Ricci contemptuously flicking a cigarette butt on a coffin as it is lowered into the ground. We don't know who lies in that coffin, but we're already hooked.

Each scene is described on the page when the producer hands the script to the director, but the director doesn't just turn the material into film. He interprets it, shapes it, gives it pace and inner life. Actors when they're given a script tend to read their parts, count the lines. The director dives in and immerses himself in a script; he'll take it home, turn off the cell phone and read it through in one take without making notes. He will want to get a sense of the story. He will then go back and read it through again, many times, looking for nuance, depth, reversals, surprises. He will need to engage emotionally with the work in order to create an emotional response in the audience. If the story doesn't move him, he should pass on it, because it will remain flat when it reaches the screen.

If the story does grab him, he will undoubtedly perceive elements differently from the writer. That's when the fireworks begin. Perhaps the female screenwriter is telling the above Firefighter's story from the point of view of the Mother whose infant is trapped in the building. The director may see the story from the Firefighter's point of view, and the entire script will have to be restructured for him to tell the story that way. Imagine *Cinderella* told from the point of view of one of the ugly sisters. How does she feel when this pretty, self-effacing waif moves into the family home? It is not necessarily a better story. But if that's the way the director sees it, that's the way it will be done.

Burt Lancaster, after thirty years as a Hollywood leading man, got to direct for the first time and relished being the early bird on set each morning; he enjoyed dealing with 'temperamental actors' and their 'little problems.' At the end of the day he was anxious to pick up the rushes and he'd spend half the night studying them. 'When you are a director you are God, and that's the best job in town.'[3]

Scripts for short films are often burdened with excess characters. The director may see immediately that the cleverly constructed lines given to the Barman in one scene and the Desk Clerk in another can be combined: it saves money and time on an extra actor, gives one actor a better role – a chance to develop that role – and those key lines are still there, the same story is being told.

This is collaboration. The writer has to accept that this is going to happen, and the director has to learn how to oil the squeaky wheel and make the running easy. Rewrites, especially after all the rewrites, are painful and a system has to be established right from the beginning. As Maureen Murray – see Chapter Two – with her smiley faces and steely cold lines picks out the best and worst in a script, it is better for the writer, and better for the process, if the director tackles each aspect of the screenplay separately: first structure and plotting, to get the overall *feel* of the piece, before moving on to the finer aspects of dialogue and visual interpretation.

Probing Questions

When the director breaks down a script, he will ask himself a number of questions:

1. What's the story actually about?
2. Who is it about?
3. Do we empathize with the main character/s?
4. Are they likeable?
5. What exactly do these people want?
6. Who is stopping them getting it?
7. Why?
8. Are there surprises, thrills, revelations: is the audience led one way before the opposite is revealed?
9. Is the audience lifted and let down and then lifted again, the peaks and troughs going higher and plunging lower as the story builds?
10. Do the main turning points and climaxes appear for maximum impact and interest?
11. Do we have the elements you'd expect for the genre?
12. Have the principal characters gone through major, irreversible changes?
13. Are those changes credible?
14. Will those changes move and affect the audience?
15. Is the underlying theme clearly revealed?
16. Is there a satisfactory ending which gives the audience what they expect, but not exactly how they expected it?

These questions should be applied to the script as a whole before the director moves on to the finer details:

1. What's this scene about?
2. What does this scene achieve?
3. Is this scene necessary?
4. What does this scene tell us about the main character/s?

5. Do the secondary characters have their own dramatic function?
6. Does this scene have conflict, a beginning, middle and end?
7. Does this scene contribute to the main character's/s' objectives, development, revelations of true nature?
8. Do the characters behave consistently, and where they are inconsistent is that understood and applicable within the narrative?
9. Do the characters have individual voices, word patterns, slang?
10. Can verbal exposition be replaced by the visual?

At the script stage, every detail can be investigated, chewed over, pulled apart and put back together again at little or no cost. It's the time to get things right. There are directors who rush into production and try to cover holes in the script once they're on set – but like the writer who's reluctant to write new drafts, this is a director the cautious producer will avoid.

Theme (No. 15 in the first list above) is the essence of the script: the fight against injustice (*The Hurricane*), the search for love (*When Harry Met Sally*), the struggle for freedom (*Gandhi*), the quest for personal validation (*All or Nothing*), fear of the unknown (*Signs*). Arthur Miller finishes a play before he is fully aware of the theme. Once he gets it, he jots it down, sticks it on the wall above his desk and gets on with writing a new draft with that theme informing the characters' decisions and choices. There may be more than one theme; John Malkovich's extraordinary if sometimes muddled *The Dancer Upstairs* (2002) blends love, injustice and the struggle for freedom.

An independent film, especially one made by a writer/director, is likely to be an exploration of ideas, an individual voice with a specific viewpoint. Most short films fall into this category: made during the time when new film-makers will be testing the boundaries of their own creativity, finding their voice. If the short conforms to genre: horror, crime, melodrama, *film noir*, science fiction, comedy, the conventions of that genre need to be observed in order to meet audience expectations. Film stories, whether they are genre-based or not, are commonly rooted in moral issues and contain lessons on how to behave in a changing world with its myriad anxieties and temptations. The conflict between good and evil is as basic to the modern screenplay as it was to the tribal story-tellers sitting at the camp fire, and people are more likely to be pondering the ethical conundrums of capital punishment, immigration and abortion on a Saturday night at the movies than they are in their places of worship in the cold light of day.

Writer Steve Biddulph argues that through television, magazines and other media, children learn values such as 'Looks are everything,' 'Your sexuality is something you trade for being liked,' 'Money buys happiness,' 'Friends will come if you have the right stuff.'[4] Celebrity, youth and wealth are the idols we have come to revere. In a splintered society shorn of the ethical cornerstones of traditional close-knit communities, movies for many have practically taken the place of religion, giving film-makers the role of moral arbiters as well as entertainers, an onerous responsibility.

Every decade is marked by its genre: the musicals of the 1930s were an escape from the Depression; the 1940s' Westerns saw stories of split families after the uncertainties of the Second World War; the Cold War and the Bomb were reflected in 1950s' and 1960s' science fiction; new attitudes to sex, drugs and rock and roll marked the 1970s; while Schwarzenegger and Stallone were emblematic of the 1980s' cult of the individual, one man against the world, a drinker, fighter, gambler, veteran, often a loser who, deep down, has the best of human qualities and his heart in the right place.

This, too, can be applied to the protagonists of *film noir*, a style that originated in the 1940s and has continued through the decades, *Chinatown* (1974), *Body Heat* (1981), *Blood Simple* (1985), *Pulp Fiction* (1994), *L.A. Confidential* (1997), *The Man Who Wasn't There* (2001) – all exquisite, multifaceted contributions to the genre.

Film noir originated with the writers and directors who adapted the detective novels of such authors as Raymond Chandler, Dashiell Hammett and Cornell Woolrich. The common theme is the dangerous if desirable *femme fatale* who challenges the values of a male-dominated society normally portrayed as decadent and corrupt. Set in a world of small-time hoods and petty, self-seeking officials, the detective central to these stories is an alienated, down-at-heel outsider who maintains a strict moral code while he sets about both solving the crime and dealing with the symbolic temptations of the *femme fatale*. Whether he succumbs or not, his integrity is never in question.

The Blues Brothers (1980) has the catchphrase 'We're on a mission from God.' It sounds both silly and unlikely. But is it? John Belushi and Dan Aykroyd are getting their band together for one last gig with Southern rednecks and a scorned woman with a rocket launcher in hot pursuit. They need money, not for a stake in some nefarious venture, but to save their orphanage. We identify with Belushi and Aykroyd, as we identify with the musclemen Schwarzenegger and Stallone, because the characters they play believe in common human decency and uphold the values of our culture.

In Quentin Tarantino's *Pulp Fiction*, Bruce Willis plays Butch, a boxer instructed by gang boss Marsellus Wallace (Ving Rhames) to overcome his pride and throw a fight. Butch, however, backs himself against the odds, kills his opponent in the ring, and picks up a fat pay day. He's about to flee with his girlfriend, but she leaves the watch passed down to him by his father at their apartment, which he knows Marsellus's men will now be watching. But Butch can't go into exile without that watch and, in returning to get it, he has to shoot Vincent Vega (John Travolta) with Vega's own gun to survive.

Fleeing again, he literally runs into Marsellus in a car crash. Both are injured and stumble into a gun shop run by neo-Nazis. Butch escapes, but goes back to save Marsellus from the torture scene unwinding in the basement. Why? It is true to his nature. Butch always does the right thing. In the boxing ring, the death was accidental. In his apartment, he shoots Vega in self-defence. He was told to throw the fight, cheat the punters, swallow his pride. But he remains proud, with the values we admire and to which we all aspire.

During the course of the story, Vincent Vega's partner Jules (Samuel L. Jackson) has seen the hand of God at work in saving him from certain death and decides to give up crime and 'wander the earth.' Vega not only ridicules this conversion, he falls under the spell of

Marsellus's wife (Uma Thurman), the *femme fatale*. As a man bereft of ethics, he is the obvious sacrifice to ensure Butch's escape. Vega is not the only character in *Pulp Fiction* to lack morals, but his demise serves to underscore the theme that, while amusing in the world created by Tarantino and Roger Avary, crime still doesn't pay. The gap between genres has narrowed and blurred – the *Scream* films are slasher comedies; *Chicago* is a crime musical; kick-ass extravaganzas and gross-out comedies will always be crowd pleasers. But while society grows ever more divisive and complex, the cinema becomes the place where serious issues are explored untainted by the hidden agendas of politics and newsprint. It's something of a cliché to say that fact is stranger than fiction. More to the point, it is through fiction that we are best able to articulate fact.

Director Stephen Frears' *Dirty Pretty Things* was enticing people out of the pubs and into cinemas over New Year 2003 with a story set among the illegal immigrants who toil at night in London's mini-cab offices, sweatshops and grubby hotels. With Chitwetel Ejiofor playing a Nigerian who trained as a doctor, and Audrey Tautou as a Turkish asylum seeker who dreams of going to America, Frears captures a cruel, creepy, paranoid city and exposes the human side of immigration as he grapples with the issues of color, race, religion and the illicit trade in human organs.

To take a horror film example, in Bernard Rose's *Candyman* (1992) the ghost of murdered black slave Daniel Robitaille returns to seek revenge on a complacent white society that has failed to confront racism. Paul Wells in his study *The Horror Genre* describes this as a metaphor on racist culture and the prevailing legacy of slavery.

> The monster – essentially a brutal avenger – is once again morally ambivalent because of the apparent justice that motivates him. Here, the arcane, primitive world perpetrates a seemingly justifiable horror which the contemporary world must confront in order to find understanding and achieve atonement.[5]

Cinema is often blamed for creating a moral vacuum with its fast-food diet of violence and pornography, but the reverse, not ironically, but typically, is also true. More than modern art or contemporary literature, cinema is the place of philosophical and social debate. A serious novel is considered successful if it sells 10,000 copies. A film director reaches millions with his movie.

The role of film, and film-makers, is not to come up with quick fixes for our anxieties and problems, to provide morals and meanings. The role is to set out ideas in new ways and allow the audience to fill in the gaps where gaps are there to be filled and, alternatively, to show that as often as not there are no simple answers.

Again, the above examples are taken from feature rather than short films and have been chosen because anyone reading this book will probably have seen those films, and should see them if they haven't.

Jenny Borgars, head of the Film Council Development Fund, told Nic Wistreich on the online film magazine *Film Netribution Network* that new film-makers need to study the work of people who have excelled in the profession. Training is only one route to knowledge, and an enormous amount can be learned by giving someone ten great American scripts that have been made into movies. The new director can study the pages, study the shots and see exactly how the transfer to screen is realized.

According to Jenny Borgars, a lot of American scripts allow the reader enough space to fall into the story, rather than trying to give the reader all the information possible. 'A writer/director needs to know what to put down on the page in order to get their film sold into the market – before they actually *make* the film,' she continues. 'That sounds like a crude distinction but it is quite difficult convincing people of it.'

While script development is an on-going process throughout pre-production, the director will also be liaising with the casting director, cameraman, storyboard artist, set director, the props and wardrobe departments and make-up, each element adding shades and layers to the dramatic effect the director wants to achieve, the story he wants to cast before the public.

The infamy of Buñuel's short films reflected his times: the left–right divide, new attitudes to sex and the church. Each generation must tell its own stories and as such the director is the thermometer taking society's temperature. He must see everything, be interested in everything and always seek truth. The Italian director Federico Fellini once said that at school he learned almost nothing except how to observe the silence of passing time, to recognize far-off sounds, rather like an imprisoned person who can tell the sound of the bell of the Duomo from that of San Augustino. 'I have a pleasant memory of entire mornings and afternoons spent doing absolutely nothing.'[6]

While he was apparently doing nothing, Fellini was meditating on his times, which he captured in *La Dolce Vita*, a film so overpowering when it was released in 1960 that critic Andrew Sarris argued that in terms of social impact 'it is the most important film ever made.'[7] It was the height of the Cold War; Algeria was fighting the French for independence; thousands perished in the Agadir earthquake, and Fellini, his eyes always half hidden under a black hat, had chronicled the spoiled, confused, aimless lives of those who frequented Rome's Via Veneto: spent writers and bored aristocrats, calculating adventurers, social climbers and the *paparazzi*, from where the generic term originated.

When the film was first released, in the cinema lobby a woman in furs waved her fist at Fellini and screamed: 'You are putting Italy into the hands of the Bolsheviks.' And a man in a dinner jacket spat in his face, the modern equivalent of challenging Fellini to a duel. As the film moved out across Italy, a civil war erupted in the media, church pulpits, in public debates and in open fights outside movie houses where the police were often called to quell a riot. *L'Osservatore Romano* described the film as disgusting, obscene, indecent and sacrilegious; *Il Quotidiano* suggested the film's title *The Sweet Life* should be changed to 'The Disgusting Life.'

Looking at *La Dolce Vita* today, it is difficult to understand what all the fuss was about. But, as biographer Hollis Alpert explains in *Fellini, A Life*, at the time, while Italians had achieved a post-war miracle, economically and socially, here was a film that implied that the miracle had been reduced to 'the shoddy pursuit of materialistic goals and pleasures.'[8] This view was not shared when the film was released internationally because Fellini had held up a mirror to *his* world, to Rome. In the reflection the Italian public saw truth and it is truth alone that leads us to greater understanding or to clench our fist in outrage.

La Dolce Vita is set among what at the time was becoming known as the jet set, but as a portrayal of contemporary society, with its naturalistic acting style and scenes shot on location, it conformed to the tenets of neo-realism, a trend that moved across Europe like a breath of fresh air and evolved with a socialist emphasis on ordinary people living tough, often deprived lives. Ken Loach's 1966 *Cathy Come Home*, for example, led to questions about homelessness and the social services in the Houses of Parliament and the formation of Shelter with actress Carol White its first figurehead. The appetite for films that make us laugh, cry and finally think about who we are and the world we live in has not diminished and accounts for some of the most successful UK movies in recent years, *The Full Monty*, *Brassed Off*, *Billy Elliot*, *Bend it Like Beckham*.

The need for stories that shed light on the fears and values of the age is as vital, perhaps more vital, now as it ever was and applies, not only to features, but to short films as well. I got the impression talking to short film directors that the ideals held dear by the likes of Loach and Fellini are undimmed and, if anything, are shining more brightly. Directing, says Cedric Behrel, is first about *having something to say* and learning your craft in order to be able to say it loud and clear.

> You must know how to use the cinematic palette to get across an idea, a vision, a character, and do so with an original, unique interpretation of subject matter. We can't expect a director to be an established writer, essayist or philosopher – he is only a vector of such thoughts, he can only be judged on his capacity to express his material with his tools, the cinematic palette of narration, drama and style. For that, he must make sure he gets the best material possible.[9]

Following the signposts of social realism, Behrel's films include the twenty-minute *Lush*, the story of a young woman repressed by her ultra-modern, lifeless environment who sets out on a journey of self-discovery; the ten-minute documentary *Who's Afraid of Vanessa SB?* with artist Tracey Emin; and *St Elucias's Island*, the story of thirteen-year-old Leah who, caught between an abusive mother and the menace of a vicious, small-time businessman, must succumb to a terrible fate or find the strength to break free.

Behrel finds a common difficulty for shorts directors is that they become *too* involved in aspects of the film that have little to do with directing: writing draft after draft, dealing with production issues, locations and so on. 'The focus necessary to direct film – and most of all, direct actors – requires such concentration and energy there isn't enough left in you for anything else,' he explains, and remembers driving the lighting van on a film school short because the director of photography (the DOP) didn't have a licence.

This has a lot to do with budget restrictions and the fact that most film-makers tend to self-finance their first attempts. Cedric Behrel's advice is to find the most competent people you can and make sure they are placed in key positions: writer, producer, director – the same opinion expressed by Alfred Hitchcock.

'In this spirit I would think it is more important for an apprentice director to have a production manager than, let's say, a camera operator.'

Behrel's Guidelines

1. Cut down on locations and try to get the locations close together.
2. Rehearse. Rehearsal time is cheap and it allows you to save time when you shoot.
3. Have post-production in mind before you shoot; what can be done in post-production should reflect the shooting style.
4. If you use stage actors (the norm in the UK), get them to 'play it down.'
5. Never shoot a script that you are not at least 300% sure about.
6. Know what you are doing: don't try and fit a specific format if you are making an experimental film and, if you are making a genre piece, know the rules and history of the genre you're dealing with.
7. Don't expect to earn money from a short.

Behrel believes that on a short film, a director needs to be persistent but flexible, ambitious but realistic. 'You must be hardworking and have vast knowledge of every component of film-making,' he adds. 'You need to be able to talk to everyone on set and be open to nuance. You must know the difference between a good take and a bad one and, more important, know what to do about it.'

Being 'open to nuance' is much the same as being flexible, which was described by Alexis Bicât as 'flashes of inspiration.'

'After all the care and planning, once you get on set, those flashes are sacred and can come from anywhere, actors or members of the crew, the sun appearing unexpectedly through the clouds. If you are not open to ideas and prepared to reverse your thinking, you will never be a strong director.'

Alexis Bicât directed *Noise Control* (discussed in Chapter 6) with *Lock, Stock and Two Smoking Barrels* star Nick Moran playing a fighter pilot. 'As far as I'm concerned, he's Britain's top indie actor and I have to admit I was nervous going on set the first day,' he explains. 'But the thing with stars is that they get where they are because they are good actors. They are actually more easy to work with because they are more technically proficient.'

How do you get a major performer like Nick Moran in your short? 'Just ask, they can only say no. And they may say yes,' suggests *Noise Control* writer Terence Doyle.

While the director assumes complete creative control and bears responsibility for any problems or errors that occur, Bicât stresses that it is essential to have a close bond with the DOP. He is normally more technically trained and will ensure basic things like the film is exposed properly. 'The film is preconceived, with each shot and sequence cut in your head, but the DOP will know whether what you want to do can be done and how to do it.'

Noise Control DOP Simon Dinsel had never filmed from a plane before and had to familiarize himself with the specially hired kit, an Aaton Minima camera and the Kenlab stabilizer that operates on a series of gyroscopes. Film can run through this small, versatile camera at forty-eight frames a second, which makes the action appear smoother when its slowed down to the standard twenty-four.

'About 95 per cent of people who go up in a training jet throw up and Simon did also,' says Bicât. 'But he kept going and got all the shots. That's what you need when you're making a short on a tight budget: technicians who are prepared to do anything. Like good actors, they are easy to work with.'

Though written as a short in its own right, *Noise Control* was planned as a taster for the feature being developed by the same team and, as such, is rich in feature production values. The film was shot on 35mm with digital composite effects (CGI); video to film transfers; Dolby digital sound mix, the twenty-nine tracks of audio mixed down to six.

'It was one of the biggest jobs on a short film ever undertaken, which resulted in us being in post-production longer than *Star Wars* waiting for downtime in CGI houses, audio suites and so on,' adds Bicât. 'It also doubled the production cost.'

Downtime means free time, usually in the middle of the night, something short film makers have to consider when they're doing a budget. Was it worth it? After being cut to eight minutes (a TV ten minutes), *Noise Control* was sold to BSkyB and secured cinema release across Wales. 'They do say a short is just a calling card for the director,' says Bicât, 'but as far as I know, all the creatives involved in *Noise Control* have added the film to their CV.'

Notes

1. John Gibbs, *Mise-en-Scène, Film Style and Interpretation* (Wallflower Press, 2002)
2. Gary Oldman
3. Burt Lancaster, in a live interview at the National Film Theatre, 1988.
4. Steve Biddulph, *The Horror Genre* (Wallflower Press, 2001)
6. Federico Fellini
7. Andrew Sarris
8. Hollis Alpert, *Fellini, A Life* (Atheneum Publishing, 1986)
9. The quotations in this chapter from Cedric Behrel, Alexis Bicât and Terence Doyle are from interviews with the author.

Chapter 4

The Editor

EVERY MEMBER OF THE production staff has a part to play in the finished film (directors Cedric Behrel and Alexis Bicât emphasized their dependence on the director of photography), but the more liberated the film-maker becomes with new technology, the more important the work of the editor.

After the director has coaxed the cast, cameraman and crew into realizing his vision, from incoherent, unwieldy footage, the story is reassembled. The director will study every shot in every sequence, but it is the editor who puts the puzzle together. All those miles of footage may contain not one but numerous interpretations of the same story and it is in post-production where the best way of telling the story is achieved.

It is a tense and exciting moment. Up until this time, the writer could have dashed in for last-minute rewrites, scenes may have been added or reshot; in Oliver Stone's director's cut of *Natural Born Killers* for DVD, punters can stay with the original and-they-all-lived-happily-ever-after final scene, or click on to Mickey and Mallory being blown away in a guns blazing Armageddon. Reviewers when the film premiered couldn't decide if *Natural Born Killers* was a bloody glorification of violence or a witty parody on American values; even the director must have had doubts to have shot alternative endings in the first place. Whether those doubts were aesthetic or commercial is hard to say, but Oliver Stone was fortunate to have the opportunity to experiment with his product in this way. For anyone making a short film or an indie feature for the festival circuit, the hard, make-or-break decisions must be made the first time round in the editing suite.

To help make those decisions, it is essential that the editor is just as familiar with the script as the director, and it should be remembered that few first-time directors will have seen a film being edited before. The director should have got the shots he needed, but if the budget precludes reshooting, errors and oversights will now be discreetly covered. Lighting, wardrobe and décor will be scrutinized for inconsistencies. Where a director may want to insert whip pans, rapid-fire cutting and wild textural flourishes, the editor like the tutor with a child genius will exercise calm and constraint.

On child geniuses, when Orson Welles was making *Citizen Kane* he became so fascinated by editing he organized a removal truck and a gang of stage hands to haul an editing machine into his hotel room. Surrounded by his actors and hundreds of feet of celluloid, he spent hours drinking whisky and learning to juggle film.

> He had discovered the Frankenstein element of film-making. Sitting at the Steenbeck, it is really possible to assemble your own creature, and give life to it. The sense of power is intoxicating: a slow scene can be made fast, a funny one sad, a bad performance can be made good, and actors can be expunged from the film as if they had never been. To shoot is human; to edit, divine.[1]

Simon Callow, quoted above, writes in *Orson Welles, The Road to Xanadu*, that Welles had discovered that in the editing process lies the ability to create as if you were God, an aspiration very close to the young film-maker's heart.

His use of sound was a dramatic advance for motion pictures and sound departments at all the studios studied his methods. Sound contributes enormously, but generally subliminally. 'Ambient sound and sound effects can transform a sequence with the simplest of means: a clock ticking, a distant dog barking, the wind, the laughter of children. Any or all of these radically alter the sense of time or place in what is perceived by the eye.'[2]

In his radio broadcast of H. G. Wells' *The War of the Worlds*, Orson Welles had terrified the nation into believing that Martians had landed. He had mastered the ability of mingling voices with effects and music and was able to apply his acute aural sense to influence the audience. 'Hitherto, in film, what you heard was what you saw. In *Citizen Kane*, for the first time, you heard something – a line, a sound – and then saw where it was coming from. The audience's mind is thus kept in a state of continuous curiosity and alertness.'[3]

Welles set out in *Kane* to create a documentary style and, with his big appetites, in this case for authenticity, in the *News on the March* pastiche showing the early life of the young Kane, he even allowed Robert Wise and Mark Robson, his editors, to drag the film over the cutting-room floor in order to get the scratched, grainy effect of old newsreels. Paradoxically, the stylization and sound effects remind the audience viewing *Citizen Kane* today that they are not watching scenes from a biodoc, but scenes from a movie. Welles had failed in his objective and made a better film as a result.

There are two distinct schools of thought regarding the editor's art: that it should be hidden, a device so seamlessly woven into the narrative as to appear invisible, or boldly present like a neon light announcing *MOTEL* on a darkened highway. Joining one or other of these two schools is fundamental to the film's symmetry, its *look*, and many directors will stay with the same editor once a style and a working relationship have been established. Ethan and Joel Coen have kept most of their cast and crew on side through a string of independent gems from their 1984 *Blood Simple* to the Oscar winners *Fargo* in 1996 and the 2001 *The Man Who Wasn't There*, shot in haunting black and white by British cinematographer Roger Deakins. *The Man Who Wasn't There* was Deakins' *seventh* Coen film – and he's done three more since.

Orson Welles never developed this collaborative chemistry, at least not with his editors. He would appear in the cutting room, usually late, study the rushes, fire off suggestions and down his whisky without offering the jug. Editors Robert Wise and Mark Robson had little affection for Welles, but they respected his knowledge, learned his secrets and, as revenge is a dish best served cold, both escaped the drawn out controversy that dogged *Citizen Kane* to begin their own careers as directors.

Where Welles had set out to imitate reality, Georges Méliès in 1902 had come to believe that reality is actually rather dull and it is the manipulation – in other words, the editing of film, that grips the audience. Before Méliès, the pioneering Lumière Brothers, Louis and Auguste, had been content to record such things as a train pulling into the station or workers flooding from the factory gates; their first public display of moving pictures was in 1895. But the interest in *le cinéma* quickly palled; there is only so much time you can spend sitting in a dark auditorium watching steam swirl about a locomotive or surf breaking on the beach.

Unlike the Lumières, whose background was in still photography, Méliès was a stage magician versed in the art of bringing rabbits from a hat and silk scarves from the palm of his hand. He experimented with the new medium by making more than 100 shorts before completing *A Trip to the Moon*, considered the first true movie. With a rocket voyaging into space, circling planets and alien life forms that wouldn't look out of place in a George Lucas film, Méliès had planted the magic seeds that would grow into the palms that edge the boulevards of Cannes and Hollywood and made moving pictures the great art form of the twentieth century. With his theatrical ability to deceive the eye by skilful intercutting, Georges Méliès can safely be described as the Father of Film Editors.

Where *A Trip to the Moon* engrossed the citizens of Paris for its novelty, the first public showing of *L'Âge d'Or* a generation later caused an uproar for completely different reasons. Film had become a political tool. The left-wing press in Paris supported Buñuel's surreal affront to religious and bourgeois values, while right-wing protestors literally broke into the theatre and ripped it apart. *Le Figaro* and *L'Ami du Peuple* led the moral panic accusing 'Judeo-Bolshevik devil-worshipping masonic wogs' for being behind the film (Marie-Laure Noailles, who in part put up the money, was the daughter of a Jewish banker). With mumblings of 'pornography' among government ministers and an official complaint by Mussolini's ambassador, it was duly banned. As Paul Hammond tells us: 'The totalitarian battle-lines were drawn.'[4]

Buñuel would have been well versed in Méliès' work and was aware of the editor's key role. He may have needed Dalí's input on his early scripts, but cut his own films, importing ideas as much from Hollywood as early French cinema. For example, a scene from Buster Keaton's 1922 *The Paleface* where the hero is embracing the girl dissolves into the same scene, the couple still in a clinch, accompanied by the card TWO YEARS LATER. Buñuel lends irony to the concept in *L'Âge d'Or* with a scene which shows a group of men in a room doing nothing in particular dissolving into an identical scene with the intertitle SIXTEEN YEARS EARLIER. Likewise, Méliès comic use of a character falling out of a window in one place and landing somewhere completely unrelated conforms perfectly to the Buñuel/ Dalí surrealist vision and was similarly borrowed. The trick, Buñuel knew, was all in the editing.

By the 1920s, film language had developed to a degree that remains virtually intact, the pace of change driven by the fact that, until 1928, film remained silent. In the theatre, the playwright can sidestep tricky plot points by having his actors tell the audience what is going on. In good writing, the skill is to *show* not *tell*, and early film-makers were impelled to use all the elements of mise-en-scène to achieve this elementary goal.

To compensate for the absence of words, silent film-makers, from Méliès in Paris to Chaplin, Keaton and D. W. Griffith in Hollywood, quickly mastered juxtaposition, parallel action, framing, lighting, camera angle, focus, filters, montage and camera movement. What the audience sees is governed by the way in which the director presents the film to us. How it is cut will determine our reaction.

None of these developments, politically or technically, went unnoticed in the Soviet Union. Before the dust had even settled on the Communist Revolution, the Moscow Film School in 1919 was already a hive of intellectual debate and experiment. Lenin, who had lived in exile in Paris, was aware of the part film could pay in educating the masses and intervened personally to ensure the wide release of D. W. Griffith's 1916 *Intolerance*, four interlinked stories showing intolerance throughout the ages and climaxing in a race between a car and a train.

A review in *New Yorker* described *Intolerance* as 'Perhaps the best movie ever made,' and it would be studied in Moscow and in film schools across Europe for its capacity to illicit strong reactions through the subtle cross-cutting of images. Griffith had come to see that there is no imperative demanding that film be presented from the point of view of the audience. He made his camera more selective in his examination of depth of field and recognized that the insertion of reaction shots heightened drama. Griffith had thus shown that in editing, the emotional result could be greater than the sum of the visual content. He was, as Cecil B. de Mille put it, 'The first to photograph thought.'[5]

Griffith began making short films in 1908, created the concept of stars and was a trailblazer for every aspect of film technique. Frank Capra once commented, 'Since Griffith there has been no major improvement in the art of film direction,'[6] and gossip columnist Hedda Hopper would recall the marks made by stars in the wet cement outside Hollywood's Chinese Theatre, and declare, 'Griffith's footprints were never asked for, yet no one has ever filled his shoes.'[7]

Flattery from Moscow came in the form of imitation. While film-making was developing in Russia, Griffith's two epics, *Intolerance* and the 1915 *Birth of a Nation*, became templates for the director's craft. What Griffith devised was the convention of preparing a shooting script to plan master shots from the camera's ideal position to stage the action in each scene. Every shot that completes the scene refers back to the master shot. In this way, he had invented cinema's unique method of treating space and provided the essential elements for editing the manifold elements into cogent sequences.

The Russians understood that truth itself can be manipulated by editing and exploited this capacity to serve the fledgling Bolshevik state. The early directors influenced by Griffith included Dziga Vertov, Lev Kuleshov and Sergei Eisenstein, whose work is studied as much in film schools today as the Russians studied Griffith in the 1920s. Eisenstein's feeling for pace and his subtle touch with actors brought a new level of quality to Russian film drama. Of his many films, he is best remembered for the 1925 *Battleship Potemkin*, particularly the Odessa Steps sequence, the sixty-second massacre of innocent civilians drawn out to more than five minutes by the frenetic cross-cutting of the 150 shots used in the scene. It has been copied many times but never bettered.

The Russian directors were obliged to glorify the state, but if film is the most powerful form of communication ever known, the role of the modern film-maker is more akin to that of the wise man in primitive societies who serves the hopes and aspirations of the community. Every anti-war story, or union struggle, or civilian massacre, is a reminder of humankind's need to learn tolerance and evolve to a greater state of humanity.

Today, it is more likely that an editor will be working on an Avid Film Composer, an editing system that stores the rushes digitally on hard disk, allowing instant access to every shot that constitutes the entire film. The machine allows the director and editor to study a variety of versions of each sequence before making a selection and, as those sequences are stored electronically, there is no deterioration during the process. Another advantage of the Avid is that both sound and effects can be tried, used or eliminated at the keyboard.

The selection and sequencing of images to tell stories has roots back to the shadow theaters of the Far East and the lantern slide shows that operated at the same time as Louis and Auguste Lumière were experimenting with celluloid. The writer and director create the material, but the editor's part in shaping the scenes into a film that remains true is quintessential. Francis Ford Coppola says a film is created three times: first you write it, second you shoot it, third you edit. The pace, timing, emotional impact, the scenes that bring a tear to our eye and send icy fingers running up our spine, with music and sound effects, the editor's job is at the very heart of the creation.

Writers put into words truths we understand intuitively and, as the writer's work goes through its metamorphosis to film, the editor is the director's conscience, the little voice that whispers when enough is enough. The finished film is in the editor's hands. Before the Avid, and before sound brought new problems with synchronization, many editors shunned the Moviola editing machines and continued to cut in their open palms, judging pace and rhythm by instinct and experience. Like the midwife whose very hands enter the most intimate of all human activity, that of childbirth, and just as writers speak of their work as being their baby, an editor when he has made the final cut delivers something new and precious into the world.

Movies *are* the culture. In 2003 when *Gangs of New York* finally rolled out into British cinemas after twelve months of delay and infighting, the disputes between Martin Scorsese and Miramax chief Harvey Weinstein were already legendary and made the evening news. Scorsese had spent thirty years nursing the project and the budget had spiralled up from $50 million to $100 million. Like the streetfighters depicted in the script, the diminutive Scorsese and heavyweight Weinstein slugged it out as the producer tried to prise control back from his director and the director ploughed on obsessively pursuing his dream.

Was the wildly ambitious three-hour epic going to be a master-piece or a bloodbath for the investors? 'I don't know,' Scorsese told Alex Williams in a *Guardian* interview. 'When I'm making a film, I'm the audience.'

Were there problems because the producer and director had a different vision, Williams asked Harvey Weinstein? 'No. Marty and I had a very similar vision,' Weinstein replied sardonically. 'We had Marty's vision.'

The exchanges are the stuff of movies and long before *Gangs of New York* even reached the cinemas, acres of newsprint drew us into the event as we followed the on- and off-screen relationship between icons Leonardo DiCaprio and Cameron Diaz, every gesture and suggestion of body language as they walked the red carpet into the premiere in Leicester Square captured by phalanxes of cameras and an adoring public. Reviews in the quality press and radio discussions examined the film's grammar, tone, complexion, every hue and mezzotint; at the outset, Scorsese had given DOP Michael Ballhaus a book of Rembrandt prints to guide the lighting, and he gave Harvey Weinstein a list of eighty films he wanted him to see including the 1928 *The Man Who Laughs*, ironically a silent movie and with the 'worst organ music,' complained Weinstein, 'that he had ever heard.'[8]

Just hype? Or a legitimate response to our major art form? In the final analysis, was *Gangs of New York* any good? Even with $100 million in the kitty and Martin Scorsese in the director's chair, it is only when the film is edited and on view that the question can be answered. And, then, reviewers and cinemagoers are going to differ. That's art.

The Buñuel Laws

Director Juan Luis Buñuel has worked with many of the masters, his father Luis Buñuel, Orson Welles, Louis Malle, Claude Lelouch, Philip Kaufman, and has come to agree with the two basic laws regarding film-making.

> 1. The first law, and one that you cannot avoid, is that there is no fixed law – no formulas, no wise sayings, nothing.
> 2. The second law is that you don't know anything about a film till it comes out. You can get the best director, the best script and the biggest stars and the film can be a flop . . . or the contrary, a bad director, bad actors, bad cinematography . . . and the film is a huge success. Or the contrary. No laws.

Scorsese's film cost $100 million, but for the mere price of a Weinstein cigar, about a hundred bucks, editor/director Sam Small not only made his ten-minute short *Passion in Pieces*, he won the Special 'Gold Remi' award at the 2003 Houston International Film Festival, and was Special Jury Selected at the 2002 New Orleans Film Festival. 'All you need is a domestic miniDV camera, a capture card, a cheap PC and a film-maker's obsession,' he says.[9]

That's just what I needed: an editor with passion.

Passion in Pieces – showing at <www.passioninpieces.co.uk> – is based on five Shakespeare sonnets, with modern urban settings and characters, and Small's own voice over. If the most important element in a film is the script, wisely he chose Shakespeare – but even with just such a wordsmith on board, Small believes it is in the edit where you make the film. 'Be prepared for a shooting/editing ratio of at least 1:50. If you work alone, shooting is a nice day out compared to the lonely weeks and months spent in front of the computer painstakingly nudging tiny clips one frame to the left and right.'

A well-planned shoot helps the editing process and before you begin, it is essential to have a good idea of what the finished film will look like. 'Cool, blue and slow? Red, disjointed and fast? Multi-coloured, madcap and fun? It may sound obvious, but the director and editor must have the same vision – and a director/editor has to be consistent.'

Small advises film-makers to *shoot everything in sight*. 'When on set or location, overshoot everything. If you can shoot the scene in yet another angle then do it. Actors, even if you have procured them for free, always like acting, so do another angle, another lens attitude.

57

MiniDV tapes are incredibly cheap, so buy a pack of ten for one day, and use them. If you only have fifteen minutes of footage for a ten-minute film you are in big trouble.'

Live sound is another key element. 'If you are using an external mike, and not shooting dialogue, then pull the jack and use the inbuilt microphone on the camera. This is almost always a stereo mike and will have excellent digital quality. The sound can be invaluable for patching silent spots with an authentic 'buzz' track, and also can be an important cue for overlaying on to dialogue tracks.' Editing is a long haul: a day's shoot can produce a month of editing. 'Rush it and you'll ruin it. Editing live footage is in some ways akin to animation. You must fit bits of dialogue and action together second by second – sometimes a fraction of a second.'

Some software can capture a whole miniDV tape and save it in distinct clips on a computer hard drive, although this fills the drive in next to no time. Sam Small prefers to watch all the takes over and over again, and then capture. As you can only use one take, it is best to do so while the scene remains fresh in your mind. 'Don't be afraid to try music or sound effects as you edit. It may help you to resolve pace and rhythm as you cut your takes. Most computer editing software has hundreds of video transitions and effects, but be wary how you use them – and never ever overuse them. Always use cut edits and very occasionally allow yourself the thrill of a dissolve or fade to/ from black.'

The value and importance of sound cannot be underestimated. Silent films always had a sound track, even if it was the local librarian playing an upright piano in the community hall. 'A truly silent film would emulate deafness for an audience and would be very uncom-fortable. Half of every film is sound, sometimes more,' says Small. "If you find that your live sound of rain on a windowpane is inferior to a library sound, then use the library sound. Don't be proud.'

In laying down sound on his own shorts, Sam Small has been inspired by Jacques Tati, the French actor and comedian who made totally original short films. To Tati, the screen was a vast canvas populated by absurd people in conflict with absurd structures. Very often a background 'buzz' track is louder than the dialogue, suggesting the ephemeral nature of conversation in relation to the natural world and to that of machines. Tati's films never contain live sound. Everything was painfully dubbed at the edit, and he would take hours to find the right car horn or door squeak. For one scene, he was once observed with boxes of glasses, smashing one after the other until it sounded just right. The music often sounds banal, but he spent months looking for the music for the effect he was trying to achieve. To Tati everything made a sound, but not necessarily it's own.

Under Tati's influence, Small suggests what he calls *casting against type*. 'Give the audience the music they are least likely to expect. Try a brass band with a sex scene. You might create a sensation,' he says. And a final warning to editors: 'Don't edit to be interesting or clever. Audiences never find *interesting* interesting, and cleverness often looks silly. What people want is to be emotionally moved by your film. If the film-maker is not moved by what he is looking at, the audience won't be either.'

The films we remember best live on because of some unique, intrinsic quality that evolves through the skills of writing, directing and editing film. As cities crumble and empires fall, all that remains through time is art. In the architecture of our churches, in paintings on the walls in national galleries, in libraries and museums, what we create is more lasting than human beings themselves. The films cited in the text, *A Trip to the Moon*, *L'Âge d'Or*, *Citizen Kane*, *Intolerance*, *Battleship Potemkin*, are all carefully preserved and available for our study and enjoyment today, long after the film-makers have gone. Whether it is that first ten-minute short or the new Coen Brothers movie shot by Roger Deakins, film's ability to change lives and minds – understood by the likes of Lenin and Hitler – is far better in the hands of artists than dictators, and in presenting truth, none play a greater role than the editor.

Notes

1. Simon Callow, *Orson Welles, The Road to Xanadu* (Jonathan Cape Publishing, 1995)

2. Ibid.
3. Ibid.
4. Paul Hammond, L'Âge d'Or (BFI Publishing, 1997)
5. Cecil B. de Mille
6. Frank Capra
7. Hedda Hopper
8. The quotations from Martin Scorcese and Harvey Weinstein are from an interview by Alex Williams, the *Guardian*, 3 January 2003.
9. The quotations in this chapter from Sam Small are from an interview with the author.

Chapter 5

Finance and Distribution

>> FILM-MAKERS AND FILM funders are locked in an eternal labyrinth. Applying for funds to make short films is the obvious first step, but the cash available is limited and the number of applications overwhelming. Funders face the unenviable task of sifting through a deluge of paperwork and, to help them select which projects are going to get this free money, film-makers with a track record tend to rise to the top of the pile.

That isn't to say that applying for funds isn't a good idea; it is. The process requires tremendous preparation, an edgy script, a compulsive synopsis, the director's statement, or a mission statement, and résumés of key personnel. This demanding combination forces the team to focus on every detail, which is exactly what a project needs whether it gets funding or not. Even with such diligence, it is important to realize that it is still a lottery, ironically so, and a good grasp on realism is the best antidote for disappointment.

In the UK by far the largest source of finance for short films is managed by the omnipotent Film Council, the umbrella group set up in 2000 under the stewardship of Alan Parker to end duplication at the various bodies formerly charged with funding and training: the Arts Council of England's Lottery Film Department, the British Film Commission, British Screen Finance, the British Film Institute's Production Department and the British Film Institute, an independent body funded by the UK Film Council to deliver educational and cultural events for the public.

With the streamlining of film subsidy and a multi-million-pound investment from the treasury, Parker and his team set out to identify the problems within the film industry and to create a framework for sustained growth in partnership with the private sector, which is largely responsible for film culture and finance. Short film-makers can apply to the four funds outlined below; full details of these and the various UK Film Council activities can be found at: <www.ukfilmcouncil.org.uk>.

- Digital Shorts: in a complete antithesis to the policy on features, which responds to the marketplace, the inclination with digital shorts is to back experimental and new media projects that exploit film as an art form; it is the training ground for new talent and shorts backed by this fund travel the festival circuit picking up more prizes than cash. Funding is organized through the London Film and Video Development Agency and ten regional bodies (contact details are listed in the USEFUL ADDRESSES section at the end of the book). Each region supports eight or so digital shorts with budgets of up to £10,000.

- Cinema Extreme: the extreme fund has been set up for film-makers with one or two 'significant' credits. What is considered taboo today soon becomes cliché and the aim here is to push the boundaries of cinema story-telling with highly contemporary interpretations of cinema art. There is a rolling submissions policy for projects of up to fifteen minutes.

- The Short Channel: in 2002, the UK Film Council's New Cinema Fund partnered with the French National de la Cinématographie in a unique *entente* to produce six short films in three pairs, each pair consisting of a British and French team making films from the same script, in English and French.

- First Light: in another new initiative, the UK Film Council's First Light fund supports eight to eighteen-year-olds with their debut digi-shorts.

Funding schemes come and go; if those detailed in these pages have since vanished, others will have replaced them. The UK Film Council encourages applications, thus the deluge, but it is not the only source of finance.

There is a growing number of competitions for first-time film-makers. The internet is the best resource to find them. Broadcasters tend to buy in most of their limited supply of short films, and then from established sales agents, but the BBC and others do finance the occasional season of new shorts and supply submission details by post and on the net. Borough councils that want to attract feature projects to their area will have a film officer in the culture department and some give small grants for short films to local film-makers, though normally for worthy rather than artistic causes.

But it doesn't matter how many competitions and grants there are, there will still be thousands of applicants for each film that receives seed money. Being turned down does not necessarily signify that projects are faulty; they may be ahead of their time. Art is subjective. Most artists need to experiment through trial and error before they do their best work, and one must wonder how many great artists there would have been had they only been given the chance.

Self-financing is taking that chance: it is the route chosen by Luis Buñuel, Alexander Salkind, Christopher Nolan and many film-makers, men and women so driven by their visions to shoot movies they grabbed destiny and a camera in their own hands and went out and did it. Self-financing requires passion and perseverance; kind, trusting friends and parents; the nerve and the ability to inspire others, small businessmen met on trains (as was the case with Salkind) or the local rich guy who fancies seeing himself on the silver screen.

A small company – or better an alliance of small companies – may be persuaded to put up some money in order to see their logo on the credits and publicity material, a mention in the local paper, a link on the website. Larger companies only show interest if there is something clear and definite in it for them. Tiffany Whittome, producer of the fifteen-minute *Homecoming*, ran a product placement company before forming Piper Films, and in her experience, if you want a name brand to put up the budget for a short film, you have to understand the marketing strategy of that brand. 'You need to have a conversation with them before you even start writing the script, you have to work with the brand right from the conception. If they feel that they are in control, they are more likely to agree to the venture.'[1]

The ideal situation, she adds, is when you cast a famous actor and the actor is willing to be associated with the brand: beer, alcohol, a clothing line, something that works within the context of the story. 'But, again, you have to be in discussions as soon as the actor is attached, and be flexible in changing the script to accommodate the brand,' she says. 'Sometimes the big car companies, like BMW, put up the entire budget for a film if there is a way that they can use the film for their own purposes.'

Some companies are more generous with goods than cash; they may supply a vehicle for a specific scene, or bowls of crisps and crates of booze for the wrap party. 'Just call the company that does their marketing, or call the brand directly. Tell them the scenario, that you'll credit them on the film, and they will have the pleasure of being associated with supporting the independent films industry,' suggests Tiffany. 'Perhaps even throw in association at festivals or screenings – especially if it's a drinks brand.'

The qualities needed for raising money have already been covered in Chapter 2, and if the UK Film Council doesn't call you in the middle of the night promising to back your opus, then the producer and writer have to sit down with their script and ask themselves some crucial questions:

- How much is the film going to cost?
- How much can we raise?
- Is there a market for this film?
- What is the USP – the unique selling point?
- Would I pay to see this film?
- Or will the making of it be an end in itself?

If the answer to the last question is yes, that the intention is to have some fun and gain experience, the goal when the film is shot has already been accomplished. On the other hand, if the aim is to sail the film into the market-place, it will require sufficient finance to achieve the quality that will ensure distribution. With a feature, it is advisable to have distribution in place at the same time as finance; in fact, a distributor will ordinarily be one of the components that make up the package. Short films, while less expensive, are more risky because it is the finished product that goes to the distributor.

There is an ever increasing number of outlets for short films, and the best of them will pick up fees when they are shown. But the principal reason for making shorts is for the film-makers to get exposure and that entails applying to festivals and entering into competition. Those that are good enough will win the plaudits and the teams behind them will be another few rungs up the ladder when they go out again in search of finance. Short films have gained a new respectability and are worthy of being considered a genre, but the ultimate goal will normally be to reach a wide audience and that can only be achieved in the long run with a feature.

One writer/director who has built her career in this way is Glasgow-born Lynne Ramsey. The UK Film Council put development cash into *Morvern Callar* (2002) with Samantha Morton and Kathleen McDermott, but only after her critically acclaimed debut feature *Ratcatcher* (1999), and her three distinctive short films, *Kill the Day* and *Small Deaths* (1996), and *Gasman* (1998). *Small Deaths* won the Prix du Jure at Cannes and when *Gasman* won the same prize two years later, people began to take notice. Lynne's shorts are moody, atmospheric pieces where shadowy, shifting worlds are seen through the clear vivid eyes of children and innocents. She has found her own unique style, her voice, and in her idiosyncratic vision funders see an originality they want to support. Lynne Ramsey's short films can be found with her features on DVD.

There is a growing trend in internet distribution for short films, the number of sites expanding worldwide on a weekly basis, and online markets are slashing the overheads for sales agents and distributors. <www.onlinefilmsales.com> provides a service for buyers and sales agents. <www.reelplay.com> is targeted at acquisition executives, investors and industry professionals; there is also a step-by-step guide to creating and editing a website, which is then hosted on Reelplay's online marketplace. <www.filmfestivalspro.com> has festival details and opportunities to make online acquisitions.

<www.filmcentre.co.uk> is an encyclopaedia for the short film-maker with cameras and kit for sale, jobs for crew, breaking news and a year by year list of short films. <www.shootingpeople.com> changed from a free to a subscription site and currently has more than 20,000 members. It is probably the best starting place for short film enthusiasts and indie features. 'An essential part of film-making,' according to Mike Figgis, quoted on the site.

Streaming shorts has become more practical with the expansion and improvements in ADSL and cable broadband. Sites come and go, but some are now established and offer useful tips for those studying the market before shooting their films. <www.in-movies.com> and

<www.britshorts.com> are UK locations with a wide-ranging fare of home-grown shorts.

The US-based <www.ifilm.com> is streaming more than 6,000 short films, with articles and festival information. Ifilm touched three quarters of a million hits with its short film *405*. After a complicated merger, Atom Films can be found at both <www.atomfilms.com> and <www.shockwave.com> – they receive about fifty films monthly in the UK, four times that amount in the US, and are constantly on the look out for 'fiction and animation with a strong narrative structure and good production values, favouring dark comedies with an off-the-wall sensibility.' The Ardman *Angry Kid* animations have knocked up more than one million hits and the AtomShockwave Corp is generally considered the market leader.

Atom has its rights structure worked out: they offer producers an advance against a percentage of gross sales for a seven-year licence period. That is not typical across the board and arrangements vary greatly. There are sites that pay small fees, particularly if there is a star in the cast, while others by contrast charge producers for showing their material. Webcasting provides an incomparable method to get seen internationally and short films do lend themselves to net exhibition. Some internet distributors, however, demand international rights, including theatrical, TV and video rights; there are problems with piracy and copyright, and while legal issues remain unresolved, film-makers would be well advised to read the small print before they sign away rights.

Self-distributors can create a buzz on a dedicated website with film clips, behind-the-scenes footage, interviews and photo stills. A site open to feedback can respond to support and suggestions, which in turn will be a useful tool in the marketing campaign and the production of a press kit. A hard copy press kit is another prerequisite and should contain the story synopsis; cast and crew lists with their experience and brief biographies; production details including the running time and print format; the details of the producer, director and writer, with interviews; and good quality still photographs that can be used for festival programs and sent to the newspapers.

While webcasting expertise is constantly changing and improving, short films are the ideal medium to get the legal and technical issues straight in preparation for the time when watching features over the net becomes commonplace. It is unlikely that this will ever be a serious challenge to a night out at the movies, but experimental and documentary features, with facilities to order copies on DVD and VHS, will have a greater opportunity to find an audience. Producer Scott Meek told *Screen International* in an interview early in 2004 that the notion that independent films with an independent spirit, made as an act of self-expression, necessarily have to open with prints and advertising in conventional cinemas 'is actually a bit like us clinging on to silent cinema at the beginning of sound.'

There are more than 300 film societies in the UK and while aficionados meet to pore over the virtues of early Eisenstein or the deeper significance of Hitchock's *Psycho*, they may be persuaded to warm up the debate with a short. Film clubs meeting in colleges and cafés offer another route to exhibition with short films being screened together with interviews with industry players and networking sessions.

The New Producers Alliance (NPA) was set up as an open access, self-help organization in 1993 under the leadership of Alex Usbourne and Jeremy Bolt. Based in London, it became an educational charity in 1995 and ten years on has 1,000 members and affiliated groups in many parts of the UK. Combined with the monthly newsletter, networking and film nights, business breakfasts with broadcasters and production companies, there are regular master classes in development, pitching, packaging, financing and distribution. With support from the Film Council, the NPA's Nine-Step Training Programme offers members a recognized qualification and NPA executives are in demand as consultants and lecturers. In April 2004, the NPA launched a members short film competition. Each month a film is selected to be screened before the feature at the monthly screenings, and from the twelve shown over the course of a year, the winning film will get the red carpet treatment at the Cannes Film Festival in May 2005. Details at <www.newproducer.co.uk>

For those who have chosen the self-financing route from the beginning they can stay on the indie trail using the professional services provided by screening rooms or preview theatres. The purpose is to sell the film to sales agents or distributors, and film-makers give themselves a better chance showing their work on a big screen on 35mm with Dolby sound and the cast on hand to lead the charm offensive. It is also a good time to invite the press and lay on some wine and nibbles for the cast and crew who have no doubt made the short on deferred payments. Numerous screening rooms are situated in Soho and charge in the region of £100 an hour, a two-hour session allowing a ten-minute short time for several showings. Theatres vary in size, seating up to 100 and as few as twenty.

It would be remiss here not to mention *The Guerrilla Film Makers Handbook* by Chris Jones and Genevieve Jolliffe, a 600-page tome published by Continuum Press. 'Invaluable insider information that gives you everything you need to know to make your movie,' wrote Matthew Vaughn, producer of *Lock, Stock and Two Smoking Barrels*, in a back-cover blurb. Visit <www.livingspirit.com> for more information. Another useful volume for film-makers looking for cash has the self-explanatory title *Get Your Film Funded, UK Film Finance Guide 03/04*, and is by Caroline Hancock and Nic Wistreich, and published by Shooting People Press; <www.shootingpeople.org>

Two organizations that should be on every movie maker's list are the The British Film Institute (BFI) and American Film Institute (AFI): <www.bfi.org.uk> and <www.afi.com> Both offer a variety of services particularly useful to those starting out in the industry. Established in 1933, the BFI has the largest film archive in the world, a vast collection of film stills and posters, and leads the field in film restoration and preservation. 'We are proud of our expertise and knowledge,' says director, Amanda Nevill, 'but while we continue to build on our reputation as a guardian of film past, we are also championing the very latest technology and encouraging young film-makers to understand the rich heritage of British Cinema.' The BFI runs the London Film Festival, the National Film Theatre on the South Bank, the IMAX Cinema.

The AFI, formed in 1967, is the pre-eminent national organization in the United States dedicated to advancing and preserving film, television and other forms of the moving image, and 'promotes innovation and excellence through teaching, presenting, preserving and redefining the art form.' With New Media Ventures (NMV), AFI has developed digital film-making coursework, student monitoring and teacher training programs in the AFI Screen Education Centre and for online film studies. The Institute sits on an eight-acre site in the hills overlooking Hollywood and is guided by four primary missions:

1. Training the next generation of film-makers.
2. Presenting the moving image in its many forms to a national and international public.
3. Preserving America's great movie heritage.
4. Redefining the moving image in the new digital era.

Memo from the BFI

The BFI offers the following advice in a free leaflet:

- Get online – from production information to sales, distribution and exhibition, marketing and publicity, the internet in an invaluable resource for film-makers.
- Have at least one very strong production still. This will be used endlessly.
- Have all clearances (especially music clearance) in place before approaching buyers.
- Make sure you allow enough time to get the film print right before your first exhibition opportunity.
- See as many films as you can, both contemporary and from the history of world cinema. Check out shorts on the internet.
- Information is power! Find out all you can about the industry by reading the weekly trade press (*Screen International*, *Variety*, etc.)
- Working at any level in the industry will gain you valuable experience. Unpaid/expenses only work experience placements are a way in.

In the early 1980s best-film Oscars were picked up by Richard Attenborough for *Gandhi* and David Puttnam for *Chariots of Fire*. At the 1982 Academy Awards ceremony, *Chariots of Fire* screenwriter Colin Welland lifted the gleaming statuette above his head and announced the onerous words:

'The British are coming.'

Trouble is, they never arrived. Up until then, before the feature was shown in cinemas, it was normal to screen a short film, the finance granted to distributors through the Eady Levy. The fact that distributors rather than the producers of short films got their hands on the grant had long been a bone of contention, although as if yielding to the auguries of Orwell's *1984*, Margaret Thatcher's government that year withdrew the levy and most tax breaks for film production. The film industry remained in the doldrums until Cool Britannia appeared a generation later and revived the business through the UK Film Council, although yet again film-makers saw one of their principal funding limbs yanked off when Chancellor of the Exchequer Gordon Brown, in the 2004 Budget withdrew tax breaks through the Sale and Leaseback scheme introduced in the 1992 and 1997 Finance Acts.

This quick, painful history lesson was learned by Kim Leggatt and Douglas Miller after they were backed with lottery money in 1997 to make the acclaimed *Princess* with Brian Cox. They had grown up seeing short films with the main feature in movie houses and their dream was to see their short on exhibition at the local cineplex. They were to discover that apart from taking films on the festival circuit, there was no practical route to television, in the UK or abroad, and showing shorts with features had become a dim memory that cineastes like old soldiers recalled as if from a golden age gone and long forgotten.

With the determination it had required to get lottery cash in the first place, Leggatt and Miller set out to revive this lost tradition. They had some success with *Princess* and learned another valuable lesson: to get shorts in the cinema they have to be just that: short, in order not to conflict with either advertising or the four or five screenings a day the exhibitors need to attain from the main feature.

During their two-year battle to get their film seen, they became a font of information for other aspiring short film-makers and set up the Short Film Bureau (SFB) in order to concentrate on distribution. They moved their operation from Brighton to London with fifty films on their books, and formed valuable relationships with Channel 4, the BBC, Sky and various overseas broadcasters. They began putting short films on airlines, they did one deal to show films at Burger King, and more cinema chains are again showing warm up shorts before the main feature.

Leggatt and Miller steered a fresh course into feature distribution in 2003, and Dawn Sharpless, SFB's former co-head of sales and acquisitions, launched Dazzle a new initiative for the sale, distribution and exhibition of short films. Dazzle is what Dawn calls a 'selective, bijou company.' After spending the last several years watching shorts, running the film club Peeping Tom's, and in Paris for Buena Vista, among others, Dawn Sharpless knows what she wants to put in her catalog and the buzzwords are quality and originality. If a film engages me then I will work with the film-makers and do everything I can to help them. It's not a financial question: I don't think, yeah, this film is going to make a lot of money. No. I have to love it. Comedy and light drama are an easy sell, but that's not necessarily what I'm looking for.

Dawn receives dozens of spec films a month. On average, less than five of them are worth seeing more than once; about one a month make it into the catalog. The best films, or at least those that Dazzle takes on, still tend to reach Dawn after doing the festival circuit. For a short film to make cinema sales, they need to be ten minutes maximum and, again, comedies sell best. Dazzle distributes a wide range of material, from fifteen-second digital micro movies to 35mm mini-masterpieces. The criteria for becoming a Dazzle film, says Dawn, is very simple: they have to be good.

How about the money: are short film-makers going to make their fortune?

She shakes her head and waves a warning finger. 'Film-makers ask: how much am I going to make? But that's not really the question. What they should be asking themselves is: how can I get shown? How can I make sure my little darling gets screened? If you make any money, you should see that as a bonus.'

Licensing fees vary: Sky at the time of writing pays £500, irrespective of length, for a three-month licence, allowing them to show the film as many times as they wish. Channel 4 pays $130 a minute for a three-year licence. Some cable companies offer as little as $50 a minute. From that, Dazzle takes a commission of 40 per cent and earns its money by helping the film-maker get their film commercially finished, helping clear music rights and then reselling the films as many times as it can.

One of the biggest costs can be acquiring music rights. Young film-makers want to use current stars to create the mood they imagine, but the cost of clearing Fat Boy Slim or White Stripes can be more than the entire cost of making the film. 'They come to me with this kind of sound track on their films and say, don't worry, no one will notice. But they will notice. If you make a film for your own amusement and show it to friends, no one will bother you, but if you want to see it screened on TV and in the festivals, you have to be professional and do everything the right way.'

Dawn suggests using original music. Composers just starting out in their career will often at little or no cost be willing to sit down with the film-makers and create the music they have in mind, even the music they admire by their rock heroes. 'But don't get too close to the original, or you'll still end facing Madonna or Eminem across the court room.'

Something a director has to learn is to leave *space* for music in order for it to be a part of the story-telling process. Music sets mood and atmosphere; it informs the audience about the nature of the characters. In Sergio Leone's 1969 *Once Upon a Time in the West*, with its sprawling twelve minutes of credits, composer Ennio Morricone uses a different instrument for each of the larger-than-life protagonists and we get to feel their presence just by a few notes whispering through the score.

A short film packed with action may need racy music, but anything with undertones and subtext will require a score that is more multifaceted, creating expectation more than thrills. In the 1970 *Five Easy Pieces*, we are introduced to Jack Nicholson as a construction worker and only later do we discover that he is railing against his musical, middle-class family. When he goes home to visit, the score switches from contemporary to classical, and when Nicholson sits at the piano to play he brings his two worlds together by hammering out Chopin's slow and haunting *Prelude in E Minor* like a piece of ragtime. The metaphor is subtle and not everyone will get it, but for those who do, it adds another dimension to the story and provides a deeper level of appreciation.

Clearing music rights for festivals can cost as little as £100. But if the film ends up a winner and you get the chance to show your film further afield, the rights issue will come up again.

In Dawn's opinion, short films in the UK are falling behind those elsewhere in Europe; she blames (in spite of UK Film Council efforts) insufficient funding for new talent. Her advice to film-makers just starting out is to go to every screening possible. 'There are festivals all over the country, the Soho Rushes festival is free, so there's no excuse. Learn the techniques, study what makes a good story and only then should people be thinking about making a film.'

Thanks to the pioneering work of the Short Film Bureau and Dazzle's timely arrival, more exhibitors are screening short films with features; some (though woefully few) cinemas schedule shorts nights, showing several in one evening; there are more TV slots, not only in the UK, but on HBO in the United States, Canal Plus in France, in Japan, on oil rigs and on numerous airlines.

Another initiative to get shorts shown with features is Short Circuit, backed by the UK Film Council and set up to create a network across the UK. As Alan Parker made clear at his first major presentation to the film industry in November 2002, a sustainable industry will need distribution-led companies in order for British films to carve out their share of the $60 billion a year world market. 'In the immediate future, we are going to have to compete on the basis of skills, even more so than costs, so we need to rapidly expand the quality of our skills base because it is the life-force that will protect the UK's ability to make film.'[2]

Expanding that skills base will mean ongoing support for short films and enterprises such as Short Circuit will ensure the work is seen. Under this scheme, the print and BBFC (British Board of Film Classification) costs are paid by Short Circuit for completed films of no longer the ten minutes that are submitted with a 35mm negative or internegative. Selected titles are offered to distributors to be attached to an appropriate feature on anything from one to fifty prints, Short Circuit striking the prints and sponsoring the PR.

Producers will be expected to deliver prints to cinemas well in advance of screening and be present for the technical check when the print is prepared for projection. Prints are occasionally damaged during projection, and the producer should check the print before it goes out to another exhibitor. As part of the UK Film Council's education program, Short Circuit also organizes one-day seminars on short film marketing and distribution, details at www.shortcircuitfilms.com

One group dedicated to showing shorts with features is Zoo Cinemas with venues in London at the Gate, Ritzy, Phoenix and Everyman, and in Edinburgh at the Cameo. A couple of hundred films a year reach them and selection is made on individual strengths and the likely capacity of a short to engage the audience and establish the tone for the feature. It is important if you want to be part of the film industry to keep up to date by reading the trade press; if you are making a short be on the look out for a feature that compliments it. Release dates and confirmed cinemas for all new movies are available from the Film Distributors Association (formerly the Society of Film Distributors – see USEFUL ADDRESSES at the end of this book).

To get short films into Zoo Cinemas, or any cinema, and many festivals, they must be supplied on 35mm. This will oblige film-makers to decide on the format when they are drawing up a budget. The cost of renting 35mm kit can be as much as the cost of buying a proficient camcorder, but then the overall cost will be much the same if the tape is then transferred to film. There are three main film formats:

- 35mm – this is the most expensive. The camera comes with bulky equipment that must be shifted around by a team on set and a multitude of lenses that can create the entire spectrum of mood and effects. It captures a clean, precise image and, with the exception of the 70mm IMAX format, for the purist, there is no other way to make film.
- 16mm – the format gained in standing after its wide use in television and, though it lacks the gloss of 35, it is still used for serious productions. A slightly larger picture area can be obtained with Super 16, used by Ken Loach, who casts non-professional actors and shoots miles of film to capture natural performances; it was

also chosen by the team behind *Lock, Stock and Two Smoking Barrels.*

■ 8mm – the Super 8 and Real 8mm are formats for those learning their craft.

The alternative to film is tape, used in a variety of DV, Mini DV, DigiBeta and HD. Tape has many advantages: it is more cost effective to produce rushes, and films can be edited before being transferred if required to 35mm.

Cinematographer Mark Duffield told an audience at a New Producers Alliance session on formats and technologies at the London Film School in 2003 that he believes high definition video (HD) will eventually supersede film and it is better to embrace the change than ignore it. Both forms, he said, have their own 'interesting ascetics' and the loyalty to film merely buys into the historic language of cinema.

Duffield shot the independent feature *Butterfly Man* on 35mm on location in Thailand and won the 2003 cinematography prize at the Slamdunk Festival – the alternative to Sundance. He has shot numerous short films using various formats and has come to see that a lot of so-called good cinematography is more to do with good set design, costumes and lighting. If those are in place, the rest follows.

'Of course there are differences: film is a chemical process, video uses pixels – it's like painting in oil or acrylics,' he said. 'People think if they shoot on 35 they will have a masterpiece. But high definition video is coming and very soon you won't be able to tell the difference. Like shooting in black and white, film will one day become a specialist tool, not the norm.'

He explained that digital grading – or *timing*, as it's known in the US – is starting to revolutionize the way films appear to the audience and how we now have a palette of millions of colors and tones to help us achieve 'a look.' Perfect examples, he pointed out, are *Amelie, Sex & Lucia* and *XXX*.

'Shooting on film or tape needs the same discipline, the same care with lighting, the same preparation, and if this is all done, when the tape is blown up to 35mm, it will be the quality of the product that matters, not the way that you got there.'

When the UK Film Council do call, it is not always to announce that there's a check in the post. On occasions, it is to invite the producer – sometimes with his director – to pitch the project to development chiefs, a skill requiring the same verbal dexterity as the street trader hawking perfume outside Harrods.

Pitching has a long tradition in Hollywood – deftly satirized in Robert Altman's 1992 *The Player* – and what happens in Hollywood arrives on UK shores with the certainty of the tide, taking on in this case a more genteel form. With executives drowning in a sea of words, memos, outlines, new scripts, second drafts, text messaging and machine gun spray over the email, a verbal pitch is an efficient way for film-makers to get their message across to potential funders in as short a time as possible – often as little as three minutes, the so-called 'elevator pitch.'

At film festivals, a more generous ten-minute pitch is common. Producers will suffer repeated rejection, but it at least gives them a chance to hone the pitch, as well as the concept, until they do find interest – or conclude that the idea just isn't going to hack it after all. One problem for producers is that ideas are sometimes 'in the air' and while what they are pitching may be completely original to the writer, it may already be yesterday's good idea to the rushed exec behind the desk.

After attending the formats session under the chairmanship of short film-maker Alexis Varouxakis, I went along to the NPA's crowded pitching and development night later in 2003 where independent producer Daniel San (*Understanding Jane*) hosted a panel discussion with screenwriting tutor Phil Parker, independent producer Phil Hunt (*Fast Food*), Parallax producer Sally Hibbin (*Land and Freedom, Carla's Song, Liam*) and UK Film Council executive Himesh Kar.

They had all been through the mill both pitching and hearing pitches and they didn't always agree on how to approach the process, but if there was a common denominator it was this: *don't* tell the story, get people interested in the idea, the lives of the characters and the hurdles they face.

'What really matters is the power of the concept,' stressed Himesh Kar. 'If you can get people's eyes to light up, you've got them. If they want to know more, they'll ask, don't worry.'

'Make your story grounded in reality,' advised Phil Hunt. 'When a story comes from the real world, or grows from a life experience, it's something everyone can identify with.'

Kar was nodding thoughtfully as he spoke. 'Be careful, though,' he added. 'Pitches that come from people who say it's a personal story, that they have lived this life, it can be interesting, but I often find it off-putting. I strongly believe in the force of the idea. That's what affects me.'

What they did agree on is the need for research: 'If you know about the guy you're talking to, it is less intimidating. It will be easier to find out if you have things in common,' says Sally Hibbin. 'Find out what people are looking for. Speak to assistants and secretaries. They are the first point of contact. They often have an overview and will know if you are wasting your time – or worse, wasting the time of the person listening to your pitch.'

They dismissed the suggestion from a member of the audience who asked whether a £50 note in a birthday card for a secretary was a good way to reach the boss.

Kar turned his thumbs down. 'Absolutely not. There's a bullshit detector that goes off when people try and manipulate the system or exaggerate, when they say they have credits when they don't, or they have stars attached when it's just a wish list. If the person you're pitching to is interested in the idea, the first thing he'll do is go on the web and check the Internet Movie Data Base to check your credits. And if you say you have a star on board, they'll ring the agent. Everyone knows everyone in this business and if you're making your way in, you have to be honest and plain speaking. That's the way you earn respect.'

As a producer who has worked with Ken Loach and has a dozen films to her credit, Sally Hibbin has come to rely on the Six Degrees of Separation theory. If you really need to reach an actor or an actress, there is always someone who knows someone and you follow the trail until you get to them. In the end, actors want to work, and if they are right for the role, and if the project interests them, they'll want to be involved.

For those setting out in their career, it is not going to be as easy as that. In a former incarnation, Himesh Kar represented writers and directors at the William Morris Agency and in his experience, agents and their assistants are very cynical. They have seen it all and heard it all and they are always on their guard. 'In the end, it's very difficult to get talent involved unless you already have the money.'

Phil Parker made the point that it is often more important in the early stages of a film-maker's career to find allies than to find money. If you are able to get an executive producer attached to a project, it may help a lot more in the long run, first to complete the package, and then to find finance. 'A pitch rarely gets your film financed, a short or a feature, but it may get your foot in the door. It may seem strange, but most people in the film industry are amazingly generous. There is a core of people willing to be mentors. They are bombarded with projects and whether or not they decide to help you will really depend on the way you approach them.'

Chair for the event, Danny San, pointed out that if you are going into the film business, you are there for the long haul. You will tend to meet the same executives again and again. You will get to learn what people are looking for, how to approach them – and when to approach them. 'You have to be so passionate about a project that even if everyone turns it down, you are still passionate. That passion is infectious. It will get you noticed.'

The Pitch

How exactly do you approach a pitching session? Phil Hunt outlines his own ten-minute plan:

1. Introductions and greetings: give your full name, company name and a business card. Don't expect people to remember you, even if you have been invited to pitch a project.
2. Tell them what you are going to talk about: a short film, feature, documentary, TV series.
3. Clarify exactly what you want: development money, funding money, the executive to read a script, to read a new draft.
4. Briefly outline your credentials and achievements.

5. Give them a chance to ask you questions.
6. Present the main elements of the story, the characters and conflicts, and why you believe this story is unique. *Do not* tell the story. Describe your target audience, any similar films and how much money they took.
7. Give an idea of the budget, funds attached, if any, and potential sales. Point out the benefits to the company you are pitching to.
8. Summarize important aspects of the package: cast, director, department heads.
9. Leave supporting material: synopsis and/or script, details of the package.
10. Thank the exec for listening to you, shake hands, and it's time to go.

Danny San pointed out that there are grave dangers in going to a pitching session two handed. 'If there is not a unified vision, they will know straight away,' he added. 'I find it best to go alone the first time and, if I am called back, I will take the director with me. Whichever way, you should practice a pitch like an actor with his lines. Collar friends and pitch a film like you were telling a true story. You have to get so familiar with the subject, you can tell it in thirty seconds or in ten minutes, and retain the same essence.'

In the same way that the £50 in the birthday card ploy is ill-advised, the panel counselled against over-packaging projects, filling pages with pictures or graphics. Many ruses have been tried – the hard grafting UK Film Council's New Cinema Fund chief Paul Trijbits admits to having once delivered a horror script to a production company in a miniature coffin. But while this might be mildly amusing, the script will have to stand up to the hype.

Parker drew everyone's attention to the importance of the written outline or synopsis that is crucial to supporting the verbal pitch. His advice is that it should be no more than four pages, and better still just one or two, and he suggested dividing it into four brief sections:

1. A premise statement, setting out the characters and what the story is about.
2. A description of the needs or dilemmas faced by the central characters.
3. A section which deals with the central crisis of the drama, leaving enough space for the executive to get involved – don't reveal the plot.
4. A statement that this will be this type of film, this will attract this type of audience – something totally positive.

Finally he explained that the major weakness he comes across is that projects are rarely what they claim to be. 'A film has to be unique *and* familiar, a mixture of both, and that is very hard to achieve.'

To return to financing short films from public funds, the competition is tough, but film-makers do come through the process and I spoke to Dušan Tolmac about his experience after being awarded £9,000 by the UK Film Council to shoot *Remote Control*, his 6-minute-and-40-second digital short about a middle-aged couple fighting over their TV remote.

As part of the award, Dušan attended workshops in script development; he took part in directing sessions with professional actors; there were lectures on the changes in digital technology and conferences with industry experts. The training sessions took place concurrent with the shooting of the film, Short Circuit handling distribution.

'There doesn't seem to be any secret about getting finance. It doesn't matter how many short films you have made, you can still get turned down. Tastes and views change on an almost daily basis,' he says. 'I have been working with the same team for three years and it was vital for the award to have the team in place; it means you are taken seriously.'

Dušan believes the secret of a good short film is honesty. 'You have to be true to yourself and true to your depiction of human situations,' he explains. 'The beauty of cinema is that the same piece can mean ten different things to ten different people – as long as it is underpinned by an essential truth, it will work for each one of those people on a variety of levels. If you approach the film honestly, the format and length and genre are secondary.'

Although Alan Parker is convinced that training is the best medicine for the industry, Dušan Tolmac has come to a different conclusion. He has seen what he describes as 'genuinely dreadful films' making it to the screen purely as a result of the persistence or connections of the film-makers involved. 'There are too many films that have nothing to say,' he points out, and he reiterates the words of director Juan Luis Buñuel: 'There are no formats, no short cuts. If films are made from the heart, with sincerity, it shows on the screen and involves the audience.'

Dušan made his first short film in 1998 and, five years later, after several shorts, pop promos and TV commercials, he was hunting down finance for his first feature. 'People say you have to learn your craft. I don't really believe that. I have never read a book on screenwriting, and I never learned to direct. People try to formulize the process, but it's not about formulas, it's about communication. As I've already said, it is your emotional input, your veracity, that will make a film work.'

He remembers that when he shot his first short he was so involved with getting the crew and locations organized, he walked out of the tube in Notting Hill on the first day and suddenly panicked. 'I had no idea what I was going to do, but you go on set and just do it, you let it happen. Of course,' he adds wryly, 'It's important that the people you're working with know what they're doing.'

Notes

1. The quotations in this chapter from Tiffany Whittome, Amanda Nevill and Dawn Sharpless are from interviews with the author.
2. Sir Alan Parker, *Building a Sustainable UK Film Industry*, notes from a UK Film Council speech, 2002.

Chapter 6

Noise Control

Noise Control *is an eight-minute film written by Terence Doyle,
directed by Alexis Bicât, and produced by Danielle Anneman
and Terence Doyle. The full script appears at the end of this
chapter.*

>> **M**OVIES ARE MAGIC. BUT to make the magic
work, the coincidence of opportunity needs the
backing of preparation.

That was the experience of writer Terence Doyle. He was
lamenting the state of his various feature projects in a pub one night
when TV director Peter Chapman mentioned that he could get hold
of a jet plane - for free. By the time his glass was empty, Terence had
made two promises: to write a feature with 'the pace of *Top Gun*, the
poignancy of *Local Hero* and the humor of *Withnail and I*,' and to
get the project rolling with a short.

Such are pledges *in vino veritas*. But he knuckled down, wrote
the short version of *Noise Control* over the coming weeks and at the
Cannes Film Festival showed it to *Lock Stock and Two Smoking
Barrels* star Nick Moran. The short, to quote the synopsis, is an action
comedy about 'a TV crew doing a story on the problems from low-
flying jets in the Welsh valleys meeting its match in the shape of a single
parent family on the ground and a heroic fighter pilot in the air.'

Nick Moran just happened to be learning to fly single engine
Cessnas in his spare time. Would he take the role of the pilot in the
short?

'Just try and stop me,' he replied.

That's movie magic.

Terence, a former journalist, had joined the London Filmwriters'
Workshop five years before to learn screenwriting. He had written
several features, and sold options on some of them, but believes he
truly got to grips with the writer's craft by working on the short.

'You come to understand the complexity of the film-writing
process by seeing what actually works and what doesn't. There are

Figure 1. The cast and crew of *Noise Control* fake Wales in a Gloucestershire garden. Photographer: Cleo Bicât.

things on the page that seem funny – that are funny – but they're just not funny on the screen. On the other hand, we found humor where it had not been planned on the page but it appeared out of thin air on set,' he says. 'So much goes into setting up each scene and you take this knowledge with you into future projects. I now look at all my past scripts in a different light and, of course, the feature based on the short embodies everything that I've learned.'

Terence Doyle's initiation into screenwriting coincided with the buzz created by the new cash injected into the lottery franchises and he has seen the opportunities for film-makers increasing ever since. There are more production companies and, even if the number of features being made has remained static at around 100 a year in the UK (more than 120 in 2004), the growth in outlets for short films has been exponential.

Most commercial shorts are self-funded and Terence Doyle had deliberately set out to write something that was commercial. 'When people go to the movies they want to be entertained; they want to see

Figure 2. Director of photography Simon Dinsel frames the shot. Photographer: Cleo Bicât.

Figure 3. Bicât (standing) readies his stars for the next take. Photographer: Cleo Bicât.

something humorous, colorful, light in tone. That's what we were striving for in the short because we wanted to keep the cast on board when we set out to fund the feature.'

Top actors make short films because they like the exposure. Everyone wants to get out and work and, if it's an interesting script, they would rather be working for nothing than not working at all. 'I imagine,' says Terence, 'the time will come when you will need a big-name just to get your short film shown.'

Not only actors, but technicians who work on features as the assistant to the assistant come into a short as the head of a department and finally get the chance to put their hard-earned skill into practice. Standards are constantly improving. More shorts are being shot on film stock with full lighting kit and high quality sound equipment. 'You can learn a lot at film school but there's nothing quite like being out there and actually doing it.'

By the time *Noise Control* was ready to roll, Peter Chapman, the man with the spare fighter jet at his disposal, was working on a

Figure 4. The cast and crew look on as Bicât (far left) directs the action on the set of *Noise Control*. Photographer: Cleo Bicât.

new project; such is the film world. Alexis Bicât switched hats from co-producing to directing and Danielle Anneman came on board as producer. At just twenty-one, the Texan ex-model already had seven years experience working on film sets in Los Angeles and London and showed, according to Doyle, the organizing genius required for the tight budget.

With Nick Moran already at the party, Danielle went through her contacts at the casting agents and signed up Gail Downey, Nigel Hastings, Sarah McNicholas, Thomas Myles, Daniel Macnabb and Søren Munk. A crew of twenty-three was assembled and moved en masse to the countryside for four days on location.

'Everyone's heart sank – including mine – when we rolled up at the youth hostel,' says Danielle. 'When actors and crew agree to work on a low budget film they know what they are letting themselves in for, but it was pretty bleak and, if we'd had more money, I would have put it into decent accommodation.'

Doyle continues: 'The first day was the brightest April day I had ever seen. It was a miracle. Then, when we set out to drive to the

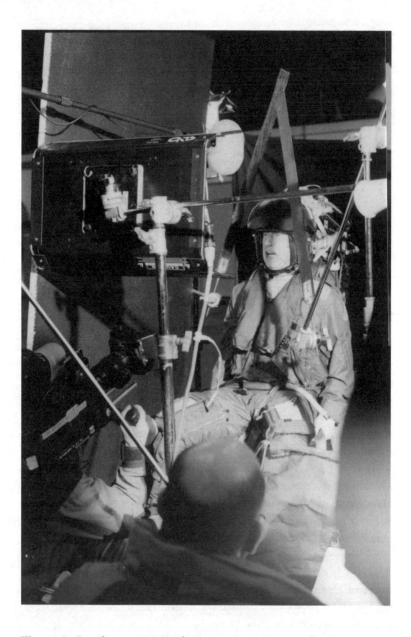

Figure 5. Leading man Nigel Hastings (center) readies himself for his final cinematic moment. Photographer: Cleo Bicât.

airport at Kemble, the road vanished as we were consumed by fog. We weren't shooting a movie. We were in a movie. It was so bad,' he recalls, 'they had to send out a rescue team to bring us in. We stood around in the hangar until about two o'clock in the afternoon, when the fog finally lifted and we started our day.'

After the ill-starred beginning, the rest of the shoot went according to schedule and 'we began the nightmare of post.' Unlike a feature, as Terence Doyle was to learn, about half the budget on a short is required for post-production. The blow-up from 16mm to 35mm (essential for cinema exhibition) is expensive, as are digital effects and the use of blue screen. *Blue screen?*

'The blue screen is literally that. You shoot against a blank screen on to which you can later project images as background. For example, you may have a couple talking in a car. You shoot that in the studio with a blue screen, then superimpose the landscape.'

There were problems with the digital effects which caused a knock-on effect in post. The company making the blow-up from 16mm failed to print the edge code numbers aligned to each frame, which meant that, when it came to adding the digital effects, it wasn't possible simply to refer to frame numbers. The special effects technician had to identify the frames by eye. This requires looking at every frame individually – and at twenty-four frames a second, that's a long and complicated business. Terence and Alexis had been fortunate to secure downtime in an editing suite at Remote Films in Battersea, and editor Brad Watson patiently cut the film together during spare weekends over many months.

Just as the budget for Martin Scorsese's *Gangs of New York* doubled from $50m to $100m, the cost of making *Noise Control* went up by the same proportion from £5,000 to £10,000. There are always hidden costs, according to Terence; even short films need end credits, then there's the cost of making videos for festivals, the press kits and postage. When you think it's all over, there are yet more unforeseen costs: in the United States, for example, they charge around $30 as an entry fee to festivals, whether the film is shown or not.

Was it all worthwhile?

There was a reflective pause, the sound of Doyle's fingers scratching his chin. Then his Irish eyes lit up. 'Absolutely. It's worth

Figure 6. The crew prepares for Nick Moran's penultimate scene. Photographer: Cleo Bicât.

it to see your characters transforming into people, hearing them speaking your lines. Seeing the story you wrote come to life is an enormous thrill, it's an education and, for me, many of the scenes look better than I had ever hoped.'

What Terence took away as a final lesson from *Noise Control* is that the writer and director have to work closely together and understand exactly what they are trying to achieve, what each thing means, the subtext, the humor and pathos. The writer and director must have the same vision and a good producer will make sure they are looking through the right end of the telescope – and at the same time.

NOISE CONTROL

A Bicât / Doyle film

Directed by Alexis Bicât

Screenplay by Terence Doyle

1 EXT. FOREST. DAY.

FADE IN: A three-man TV crew – INTERVIEWER, CAMERA-
MAN and SOUNDMAN (nickname BIG EARS)– is rushing
through a dense forest. They can't be seen clearly.
Close-ups only of the branches ahead and their
pounding feet as they run puffing and panting and
swearing. Suddenly the Interviewer breaks out into
open sunshine. He struggles to make himself stop
. . . there is obviously some kind of drop.

> **INTERVIEWER**
> Whooaa.
> (*he turns*)
> Careful . . . There's a cliiii . . .

The Cameraman thunders up behind the Interviewer
and doesn't manage to stop in time. He bumps into
the Interviewer. The Interviewer falls off screen
with a yelp. The crew stop at the top of a preci-
pice and look up, wondering where the Interviewer
is. The cameraman admires the sheer drop, he holds
the camera over the edge, then moves it back and
forth, admiring the stomach churning effect. No
sign of the interviewer yet.

> **CAMERAMAN (O.S.)**
> Nigel . . . ??? Nigel . . . . ???? Nigel ????

> **INTERVIEWER (O.S.)**
> (*ruffled*)
> Will someone give me a hand . . . !!?

The camera whip pans right to reveal the interviewer pulling himself back to safety. The Cameraman hurriedly puts his camera down facing in the

opposite direction into the woods. We see a
beautiful 'Chinese Angle' view of nature. Dappled
sunlight streams through the forest canopy and the
delicate chirping of birds is set against the
gentle movement of the trees. Off screen we hear
the crew helping the interviewer up.

> **INTERVIEWER (O.S.; CONT'D)**
> Alright. Alright. Get off. Get off.
> (*panting, beat*)
> Okay, this is good. We'll set up here . . .
> (*Breaks off, with a chunky throaty smoker's
> cough*) . . . I've got to give up these sodding
> nature gigs . . . (*more coughing*)

The Cameraman has started to fiddle with the
camera, which affects our beautiful view of the
forest. He straightens up the shot, zooms
slightly, focuses and perhaps tries a different
filter.

> **BIG EARS (O.S.)**
> Gotta give up the fags first.

> **INTERVIEWER (O.S.)**
> Alright genius.
> (*Pause for cough;
> calls to Cameraman*)
> Fred.
> (*beat*)
> Hey, Fellini.

Finally the camera jerks around from the forest to
focus on a full body shot of the Interviewer, an
ageing media 'still-trying-to-be-star' looking
ridiculous in the latest tracksuit.

> **CAMERAMAN (O.S.)**
> (*faking Italian accent*)
> Pleasea, you cana calla me Federico.

The camera crash zooms in on Interviewer's face to focus and crash zooms out to frame him in a very media friendly and convincing manner.

> INTERVIEWER
>> Sure . . .
>>> *(fake Italian accent)*
>> When you starta bringa me zee women . . .
>>> *(beat, normal voice)*
>> Ready, Ears. Sound check . . .
>>> *(Beat, exaggerated presenter voice)*
>> . . . Good morning, this is . . . *(clears his throat, tries again)* . . . Good morning, this is . . . *(another pause, more coughing, really throaty)* . . . Good morning, this . . . Okay, that's good.
>>> *(He snaps into presenter mode)*

> We have come to this pristine North Wales valley to report on one of the great evils of our time. Listen for a moment to the incredible silence around me . . .

He pauses to allow his audience to hear, and for a moment, there is absolute silence.

> INTERVIEWER (CONT'D)
>> *(to the crew)*
>> Scary, isn't it, lads?

Then there is a shrieking sound in the distance.

> INTERVIEWER (CONT'D)
>> What the . . .

He breaks off as a low-flying jet rips past, its engines shaking the microphone.

CUT TO:

2 EXT. COCKPIT VIEW OF THE VALLEY SWEEPING PAST. DAY.

> **PILOT (O.S.)**
> There is an adrenaline rush.
> (*beat*)
> That's not why I fly . . . the buzz, the
> thrill, whatever . . . It's there but . . .
> this is serious business. Simulated Attack
> Profile.

> CUT TO:

3 EXT. BACK GARDEN, WELSH FARMHOUSE. DAY.

Laundry on a line - white in the wind. The sound
of a BOY and a GIRL, eight and ten, playing
idyllically with simple toys while their MOTHER
sorts clothes. The TV crew arrive and dodge
through the laundry.

> **INTERVIEWER**
> Excuse me . . . Hello, good morning . . .
> Yes, hello.

The camera shocks the Woman. She backs away and
fusses with her hair.

> **INTERVIEWER (CONT'D)**
> Don't be embarrassed. You look . . . you
> look. . .
> (*beat*)
> We're doing a programme on the effects of
> low-flying jets on the valley. I wonder if
> you would tell us about their effect on
> your life?

The Woman looks around confused. The kids begin to chatter in the background.

> WOMAN
>
> The jets?

> INTERVIEWER
>
> The low-flying jets. Listen, right now, it is blissfully quiet here.

He pauses to take in the silence . . . and the air is filled with shrieks as the kids suddenly start yelling.

> LITTLE GIRL (O.S.)
>
> No he's not.

> LITTLE BOY (O.S.)
>
> Yes he is.

> LITTLE GIRL (O.S.)
>
> Shut up you're a little pratt.

> INTERVIEWER
>
> Hey, can you keep it down for a minute?
> (beat)
> Hey. . . Can somebody get those kids. . .

The kids are suddenly quiet, smothered by the crew.

> INTERVIEWER (CONT'D)
>
> (sigh)
> That's better. Now. . .

It is beautiful again, the laundry flapping in the breeze.

> INTERVIEWER (CONT'D)
>
> (mock enthusiastic)
> It's wonderful, isn't it?

                    WOMAN
What?

                    INTERVIEWER
          (*impatiently*
          stressing)
The peace. The quiet. The tranquillity.

                    WOMAN
Are you from a television station?

                    INTERVIEWER
          (*laboriously*
          explaining)
That's right. We're doing a piece, on the
impact of modern life in the valley.

The Woman starts primping again.

              INTERVIEWER (CONT'D)
You look er. . . You look. . .
          (*beat*)
Now can you please tell me about the
negative effects of these jets on your
simple lifestyle?

The Woman looks at him for a long time as if she has
no idea what he means; then.

                    WOMAN
          The jets?

                    INTERVIEWER
That's right.

Another long moment of waiting.

                    WOMAN
          (*finally*)
You're right, of course. There are
jets. . .

Again there is the hornet's shriek of a jet in the distance, growing rapidly louder.

> **WOMAN (CONT'D)**
> There are . . . (*her words are drowned out*)

> **INTERVIEWER**
> (*overlapping*
> *screaming*)
> Oh, not now.

Even he is drowned out. Then the plane is passed and there is silence again.

> **INTERVIEWER (CONT'D)**
> Ears, did we get any of that, Ears? . . .

Ears shakes his head solemnly.

> **INTERVIEWER (CONT'D)**
> Bloody hell . . .
> (*to Woman*)
> Could you say that again, please?

> **WOMAN**
> I said, there are planes but you get used to them. They become part of the background. They don't bother us.

CUT TO:

4 EXT. VIEW FROM THE COCKPIT AGAIN. DAY.

More scenery sweeps rapidly past.

> **PILOT (O.S.)**
> I know some people aren't happy. But when you're doing Mach 2 at a hundred and fifty

feet you don't start worrying about peace
in the valley.

CUT TO:

5 EXT. BACK GARDEN, WELSH FARMHOUSE. DAY.

Close-up on the beautiful Little Girl in a pink
dress, smiling.

> INTERVIEWER
> Can you tell me about the effects of these
> low-flying jets on the valley?

The Girl smiles beguilingly. Suddenly we hear the
Soundman make an impression of an approaching jet.

> INTERVIEWER (CONT'D)
> (*believing the
> sound to be real*)
> No.

The Interviewer realises it is Big Ears playing a
prank. He leans into shot and looks off-screen
left. We see his face clearly.

> INTERVIEWER (CONT'D)
> (*frustrated*)
> You think that's funny?

The Interviewer walks across the shot and exits
frame left, we hear a thump and the boom falls
through the shot crashing to the ground in front
of the girl, completely unfazed. The Interviewer
walks back to his first position.

>   INTERVIEWER (CONT'D)
>   (to Girl)
>   I'm so sorry about that.
>   (to Ears)
>   Ears. Come on. Come on. Pick it up.

The boom slowly rises up through the shot shaking
as it goes. The Girl smiles sweetly all the time.

>   INTERVIEWER (CONT'D)
>   Right. Going again.
>   (to Little Girl)
>   Would you say that the jets are a negative
>   influence on the quality of your idyllic
>   life?

The Girl has been waiting for this interview all
her life and she knows how to use a camera.

>   LITTLE GIRL
>   I want to be a supermodel. And I want to
>   live in a big house in the city.

Interviewer laughs artificially.

>   INTERVIEWER
>   How sweet . . .
>   (aside)
>   Give me a call when you get there . . .
>   (beat)
>   But, can we talk about the jets for a
>   moment?

The Girl pauses, smiles beguilingly.

>   LITTLE GIRL
>   I want to make a lot of money and travel
>   around the world and have men at my feet.

Interviewer chuckles again. Then lets out a sigh.

> INTERVIEWER
> But the jets . . . Can we please. . .

There is the hornet's shriek of a jet quickly approaching.

> INTERVIEWER (CONT'D)
> (*continues, looking skyward*)
> Oh . . . for Christ's sake. . .

The jet drowns him out. And he walks off screen fed up.

>> CUT TO:

6 EXT. TARMAC, JET AIRPORT. DAY.

The Pilot approaches his jet and about-faces to speak to camera. His helmet is off held under his arm. He is a handsome twenty something, smiling and ingenuous.

> PILOT
> There's no permanent damage. We come. We go. A couple of seconds. Ba-Boom. We're gone in a flash. Who can complain about that?

>> CUT TO:

7 EXT. BACK GARDEN, WELSH FARMHOUSE. DAY.

Close-up on the second child, an impish Little Boy with red hair and freckles.

                    INTERVIEWER (O.S.)
               (*tiring now*)
          Can you tell us about the effects of these
          low flying jets on your life?

A long hold on the Little Boy's face, as if he is
never going to speak.

                    INTERVIEWER (O.S.; CONT'D)
               (*continues, an edge
               to his voice*)
          Go on. Say whatever you like.

The Boy pauses as if forever.

                    INTERVIEWER (O.S.; CONT'D)
          Well yes well..?

The Boy hesitates, then finally.

                    LITTLE BOY
          I can say whatever? Really?

                    INTERVIEWER (O.S.)
          Yes.
               (*beat, irritated*))
          . . . Just get on with it.

His silent face again. Again we hear the screech
of an approaching jet. The Interviewer gives up.

                    INTERVIEWER (O.S.; CONT'D)
          Right that's it. I've. . . (*breaks off*)

The jet gets louder.

                    LITTLE BOY
               (*screaming, excited
               by the sound*)
          I want to be a pilot. I want fly a jet
          plane. And touch the stars. . .

The jet roars by overhead, drowning him out.

CUT TO:

8 EXT. VIEW FROM COCKPIT AS PLANE FLIPS UPSIDE DOWN. DAY.

The plane flips upside down. The landscape is inverted.

> PILOT (O.S.)
> You want to know what I really think?

> INTERVIEWER (O.S.)
> (*strained by being upside down*)
> Yes. Yes. Please.

> PILOT (O.S.)
> You want to know where I really stand?

> INTERVIEWER (O.S.)
> (*about to puke*)
> Please tell me. Please. Quick.

> PILOT (O.S.)
> I'll tell you. . . Up here it's you and the machine. In combat. . .

Suddenly there is an ominous rattling sound.

> PILOT (O.S.; CONT'D)
> What the..?

> INTERVIEWER (O.S.)
> What was that?

The plane rights itself.

> PILOT (O.S.)
> Pan, pan, pan. This is Blackjack five.
> I've got a problem. Engine down.

> INTERVIEWER (O.S.)
> Is that a bad thing?

> PILOT (O.S.)
> Requesting 'Nearest Suitable', over.

The landscape flashes by, but in an oblique, jerking manner now.

> CONTROL (O.S.)
> Blackjack five. This is London Control.
> 'Nearest Suitable' Five four two seven North.
> Zero six three four East.

> PILOT (O.S.)
> Copy that.

The Pilot looks at the cockpit indicators to see them all turn red one by one.

> PILOT (O.S.; CONT'D)
> This is very bad.
> (*beat*)
> Mayday, Mayday, Mayday. Blackjack five preparing to eject.

> INTERVIEWER (O.S.)
> I don't want to eject.

> PILOT (O.S.)
> Blackjack five going down right now.
> Altitude 500 feet and falling. 400. 300.
> (*to interviewer*)
> . . . We're gonna eject mate. Just like the drill . . . Are you ready.
> (*beat*)

Ready.
(*beat*)
Now! Eject! Eject! Eject!

        INTERVIEWER (O.S.)
    Eject! Eject! Eject!

The canopy blows off and there is a sudden swoosh
. . . but something is wrong . . . the Pilot has
ejected but the Interviewer is still in the
cockpit. He holds his broken ejection cord.

        INTERVIEWER (CONT'D)
        (*frantically*)
    Eject! Eject! Eject!

The Interviewer looks incredulously at the broken chord
from his ejection device that has come away in his
hands leaving him stranded.

        INTERVIEWER (CONT'D)
    Hey.
        (*looks up*)
    Come back here. My seat is stuck. Hey.

                        CUT TO:

9 EXT. BACK GARDEN, WELSH FARMHOUSE. DAY.

The Little Boy is standing in the garden, looking
skywards, frozen in horror as the jet falls towards
him. MS contra zoom of the Little Boy.

        LITTLE BOY
    Oh Muuuuuuuu. . .!
                        CUT TO:

10 INT. COCKPIT.

ECU of Interviewer's face shaking violently with the jet. He sees the Little Boy through the windscreen. He utters his last words.

> INTERVIEWER
> Oh no it's that family again!
> (he screams)
> Nooooooo. . .!

CUT TO BLACK . . . A SINGLE BIRD CHIRPING . . . MAIN END CREDITS . . . THEN

CUT TO:

11 EXT. SOMEWHERE NEAR BACK GARDEN. DAY.

The Little Boy (blackened by the explosion) staggers into a shot from a camera positioned in a tree. There is some smouldering wreckage.

> LITTLE BOY
> (*yelling excitedly*)
> Hey . . . Mum, Sis., Over here! Come on. Quick. The pilot's stuck in a tree. . .

The Little Boy looks up admiringly into the tree.

> LITTLE BOY (CONT'D)
> Can I have your autograph?

FADE OUT

Note

1. The quotations in this chapter from Terence Doyle and Danielle Anneman are from interviews with the author.

Chapter 7

G.M.

G.M. is an 8½-minute film written and directed by Martin Pickles, and produced by Kate Fletcher.

>> THIS SURREALIST FILM IN which an Edwardian gentleman is tormented by spirits who appear through holes in his sitting room wallpaper was inspired by the work of Georges Méliès and was timed to coincide with the 100th anniversary of the film pioneer's first screening of *Le Voyage dans la Lune (A Trip to the Moon)*.

Though a period drama, it makes use of the latest digital post-production techniques to create 'a modern silent horror film about birth, sex and death,'[1] and bridges time from the artisan magic of Méliès' short films to the digital magic of today. *G.M.* was made with a £15,000 grant from the London Production Fund, Martin Pickles' first film to receive formal industry backing.

It had taken a long time for Martin to get funding because his wonderfully eccentric films are neither dramas in the conventional sense, nor suitable as gallery installations. Pigeon-holing projects is clearly more an obsession in the UK and, up until the time when *G.M.* started to get noticed, his shorts found better response elsewhere in Europe.

Martin came to film-making after studying classics and, following a childhood enthusiasm for drawing cartoon strips, went from Oxford to art school to study fine art. In his mid-twenties he was still not qualified to do very much at all – he comes, he says, from a long line of late starters – and finally did something practical: a course in computer art which led to a job as a designer. By then, he had started experimenting with a super 8 camera and discovered his passion for film.

With a borrowed camcorder, he made the five-minute *Shaving*. Inspired by surrealist painter René Magritte, it shows a man getting up in the morning, putting on shaving foam and carefully shaving off his face. He sprays on a suit with an aerosol, places a bowler hat on his head and goes faceless through his day. In order to achieve this effect, Martin and graphic designer Jonathan Mercer had to repaint the film frame by frame on computer, using the PhotoShop program, a task performed in their spare time and which took nine laborious months to complete.

Shaving had cost £500 (as an artist, Martin Pickles didn't factor time in the budget); the film won a prize at the Ars Digitalis Festival in Berlin, was screened on Channel 4, ITV, at various festivals and was acquired by Canal+ in France for £1,600 putting the project suddenly into profit. A shortened version was taken by the Berlin metro to amuse passengers between stations in a scheme launched in 2003, giving the film an unexpected new life and commuters the chance to save their daily papers for the coffee break.

After *Shaving*, Martin stayed his course with experimental films. He shot a pair of short, commercial comedies, but climbed straight out of the mainstream, dried himself off and concluded that, for him, it was more important to make the sort of films he wanted to make, surreal, eclectic and without compromise. He also came to realize that, paradoxically, by keeping the day job and self-funding his films, he had been taking the easy option, and validation of his work, particularly at home – often the hardest market – would require proper funding, a professional shoot, trained crew and actors, and a more businesslike approach.

While thinking through this conundrum, Martin happened to be reading a book about the working methods of Georges Méliès. He dreamed that night that he was at a film festival and saw snatches from a short silent film. He woke up feeling annoyed that he had not seen it all and, as if guided by the hand of Freud, jotted down what he remembered. The next day, he wrote the first draft of *G.M.* 'I don't want people to think I'm completely mad, but it really happened like that, in a dream, and I knew it was the one.'[2]

Martin had already discussed his ideas with Angie Daniell and Kate Fletcher at the pop-promo production company Momentum Video. They had advised him to research what funding schemes were available, locally and nationally, and to make a habit of applying to them regularly. He still doubted that a funder would back this off-the-wall project but, remembering Kate and Angie's advice, started sending out proposals anyway. One important thing he discovered was that when you have to justify why your film is good enough to deserve public money, the discipline crystallizes the concept, you start to see it from the audience's point of view and, if there are holes in the script, you're more likely to find them.

G.M. is in fact full of holes, characters and objects appearing and disappearing through holes, characters seeing themselves through holes, but the point is clear. Martin knew he wasn't nursing a slick, commercial idea and put as much effort into writing the proposal and drawing the storyboards as he had previously put into the entire productions of his guerrilla films. His former modus operandi had been to get out and start shooting from the hip, but when the award finally came through from the London Production Fund, a scheme run by the LFVDA, now Film London, he controlled that urge and asked Kate Fletcher, who'd liked the idea from the outset, to nurture the project (read: Martin P.) as his producer.

While Kate began to organize the crew, cast, equipment, studio hire 'and the entire universe of logistical issues,' Maggie Ellis at the LFVDA worked with Martin to further develop and refine the script. 'Even if the whole thing is in your head, the rewrites and discussions clarify the concept and make it easier when you get on set.'

They had enough money for a three-day shoot at the Bow Road Studios. Paul Nash was brought in as DOP, John Pattison wrote the music score, and actors Neil Edmond, Leslie Cummins and Isabel Rocamora filled the three roles. Martin was free for the first time to concentrate on his work directing and came to realize that when you move away from low-budget productions, the specialized skill of a producer is not just advisable, but essential.

The film required a number of trick shots, including the lead actor playing two characters at the same time. With only three days to shoot, they got behind on the first two days and Martin had to work out what shots he could afford to sacrifice on the third day in order to wrap with the film complete. 'Even if my film is not to everyone's taste, it has the production values I wanted and it is at least the best possible film I could have made.'

G.M. was shot on Digi Beta, the tape format used in most TV production, and was transferred to VHS for the rushes. The VHS copy was burnt with the timecode reference from the mastertape visible on screen, allowing Martin to select the takes and make a preliminary edit on paper with the timecode references. Editor Brian Marshall digitized the rushes using the computer editing system Discreet Edit, and made an assembly edit based on Martin's paper edit. Martin used *After Effects*, another useful program, for the special effects and to retint the frames.

In the editing process, they had used similar effects and stylization to those pioneered by Méliès, albeit in a different form. Méliès would have teams of people hand-painting his film. Martin painstakingly tinted his film digitally in order to get a feeling of being removed from the real world, without merely creating a pastiche.

The film, after months of slow, intricate work in post, was completed in summer 2001. Kate Fletcher and Maggie Ellis then had to persuade Martin to take a minute out of the centre of the film to give it more pace. 'I would probably not have seen the need to do this myself, but they were right, and I did it.'

It required another grant to get the film blown up on to 35mm – essential, according to Martin, to give a 'seal of legitimacy.' Only on 35mm can a film go into cinemas and many of the festivals, which is where *G.M.* began its journey, first at the London Calling screenings at the London Film Festival in November 2001. The British Film Institute added *G.M.* to its listings as sales agent and took it to the festival at Clermont-Ferrand; it was shown at the Dalí Universe, at the old County Hall on the South Bank, and several more festivals across Europe. Cut to 8½ minutes, the film is the perfect fit for festival and TV schedules.

Drawing on inspiration from Méliès, Buñuel and the painters Magritte, De Chirico and Dalí, Martin Pickles has stuck to his own vision. He has come to see film-making as a multi-skilled pursuit and, if you haven't been to film school, it is useful to bring other life experiences to your work. In Martin's case, reading classics, studying art, drawing cartoons and mastering computer techniques combined in a surreal way with his Méliès dream for him to find a story that Joseph Campbell would have said was always there, waiting to be found.

If you track Martin's course through the firmament, as an astronomer may track the orbit of a new star, it is his single-pointedness and a belief in his own vision that have got him noticed. When the TV production company Talk Back was making a series of sketches in a Victorian style, Martin got his first industry commission as a director.

He is still, however, creating shorts, animation and new media work. He sees the short film is an art form in its own right and his style of film-making suits the genre.

'Short films can pursue one topic, be single-minded; they can be experimental, which is hard to sustain over ninety minutes.'

I caught all the enthusiasm of the perennial university student in his tone and guessed that a feature was now on the agenda.

'It's the inevitable next step. I am working on a comedy with another writer,' he explains. 'I have always made films to please myself and could not work on a film that I didn't completely believe in. All my sensibilities are contained in the feature, but it is my co-writer who brings me back into the real world.'

G.M.

or 'The Sitting Room'

A proposal for a short film
by Martin Pickles ©1999

67 Ballater Road
London
SW2 5QX

Rapid Productions
21/25 Goldhawk Road
London
W12 8QQ

Figure 7. Storyboard for *G. M.* Artwork by Martin Pickles.

G.M. Storyboard
Martin Pickles 1998

Scene 1.1
__Int.   Sitting room. Day.__
G.M sits at the table, finishing a light lunch and reading the paper. He rings a hand bell and his HOUSEKEEPER enters the room and picks up his tray.

Scene 1.2
__Int.   Sitting room. Day.__
Two shot of the HOUSEKEEPER and G.M. He thanks her for his lunch and she takes the tray away.

Scene 1.1 continued
__Int.   Sitting room. Day.__
The HOUSEKEEPER exits the room and GM stands in the middle of the room allowing his lunch to settle. He looks round at the clock to see what time it is.

Scene 1.3
__Int.   Sitting room. Day.__
Close up of old clock on the back wall: It reads one minute to twelve.

Scene 1.1   continued
__Int.   Sitting room. Day.__
G.M. examines his pocket watch.

Scene 1.4
__Int.   Sitting room. Day.__
G.M.'s point of view: we see a close up of G.M.'s hand holding his pocket watch. It says a quarter past one.

PAGE I.

Figure 7. (Continued.)

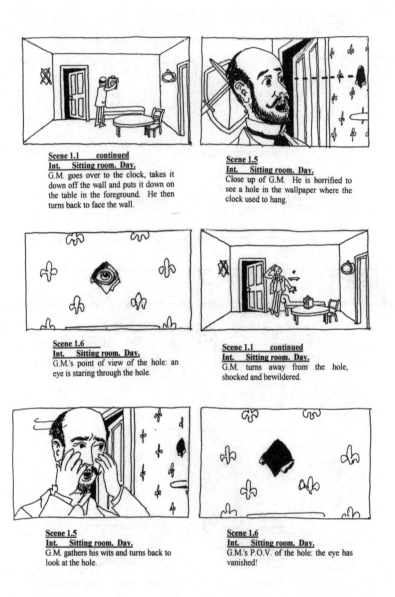

Scene 1.1   continued
Int.   Sitting room. Day.
G.M. goes over to the clock, takes it
down off the wall and puts it down on
the table in the foreground. He then
turns back to face the wall.

Scene 1.5
Int.   Sitting room. Day.
Close up of G.M. He is horrified to
see a hole in the wallpaper where the
clock used to hang.

Scene 1.6
Int.   Sitting room. Day.
G.M.'s point of view of the hole: an
eye is staring through the hole.

Scene 1.1   continued
Int.   Sitting room. Day.
G.M. turns away from the hole,
shocked and bewildered.

Scene 1.5
Int.   Sitting room. Day.
G.M. gathers his wits and turns back to
look at the hole.

Scene 1.6
Int.   Sitting room. Day.
G.M.'s P.O.V. of the hole: the eye has
vanished!

PAGE 2

Figure 7. (Continued.)

116

Scene 1.5 continued
Int. Sitting room.   Day
G.M. tries to look through the hole.

Scene 2.1
Int.   Inside wall.   Day.
View from inside the hole looking out:
we see G.M. looking into the darkness.

Scene 3.1
Int.   Sitting room. Day.
Close up of the hole from G.M.'s point
of view. We slowly zoom into the
hole.

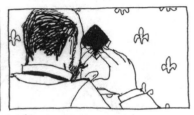

Scene 3.2
Int.   Sitting room. Day.
Over-shoulder shot: G.M tries to tear at
the sides of the hole to make it bigger.

Scene 3.2   continued
Int.   Sitting room. Day.
G.M. doesn't enlarge the hole but
instead pushes it along the wall.

Scene 3.3 (as 1.1)
Int.   Sitting room. Day.
We return to the wide covering shot of
the room: G.M. pushes the hole right
along the back wall.

PAGE 3

Figure 7. (Continued.)

Scene 3.4
Int.   Sitting room. Day.
G.M.'s P.O.V.: close up of the hole.
G.M. sees a GIRL's face inside the
wall.

Scene 3.5
Int.   Sitting room. Day.
Close up of G.M. from the hole's point
of view. We see his shocked reaction.

Scene 3.6
Int.   Sitting room. Day.
A wider shot of the hole: the GIRL's
face disappears into the darkness as a
shadow passes in front of her.

Scene 3.5 continued
Int.   Sitting room. Day.
G.M. leans forwards to look deeper
inside the hole: he is very distraught.

Scene 3.7 (similar to 3.6)
Int.   Sitting room. Day.
G.M. tears the hole open with his
hands.

Scene 4.1
Int.   Inside wall. Day.
We see G.M. as seen from inside the
wall. He rips at the wallpaper and
stares inside.

PAGE 4

Figure 7. (Continued.)

118

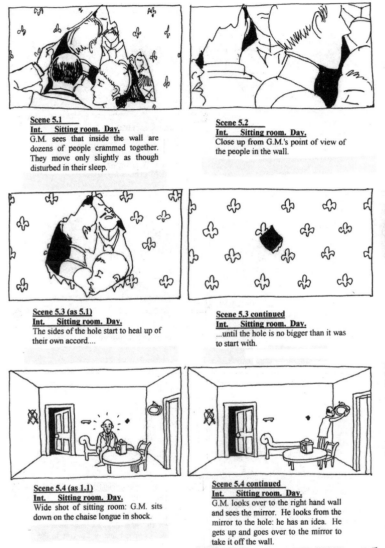

Scene 5.1
Int.   Sitting room. Day.
G.M. sees that inside the wall are
dozens of people crammed together.
They move only slightly as though
disturbed in their sleep.

Scene 5.2
Int.   Sitting room. Day.
Close up from G.M.'s point of view of
the people in the wall.

Scene 5.3 (as 5.1)
Int.   Sitting room. Day.
The sides of the hole start to heal up of
their own accord....

Scene 5.3 continued
Int.   Sitting room. Day.
...until the hole is no bigger than it was
to start with.

Scene 5.4 (as 1.1)
Int.   Sitting room. Day.
Wide shot of sitting room: G.M. sits
down on the chaise longue in shock.

Scene 5.4 continued
Int.   Sitting room. Day.
G.M. looks over to the right hand wall
and sees the mirror. He looks from the
mirror to the hole: he has an idea. He
gets up and goes over to the mirror to
take it off the wall.

PAGE 5

Figure 7. (Continued.)

119

Scene 5.5
Int.   Sitting room. Day.
Close up of G.M. and the mirror:
G.M. reaches for the mirror whilst
looking at his own reflection.

Scene 5.5 continued
Int.   Sitting room. Day.
G.M. takes down the mirror to reveal a
bigger hole.   Inside the hole a face
grins back at him: an evil parody of
himself! (This is 'M.G.')

Scene 5.4 continued
Int.   Sitting room. Day.
G.M. drops the mirror in alarm and
looks down at it.

Scene 5.5 continued
Int.   Sitting room. Day.
When G.M. looks back at the hole the
evil face has vanished.

Scene 5.6 (as 1.1)
Int.   Sitting room. Day.
Wide shot of sitting room: G.M stares
into the hole unaware that M.G. is now
hiding behind him in the room.

Scene 5.6 continued
Int.   Sitting room. Day.
G.M. stares deeper into the hole,
unaware of events in the room. M.G.
crawls under the table and the GIRL
starts to climb out of the hole in the
back wall.

PAGE 6

Figure 7. (Continued.)

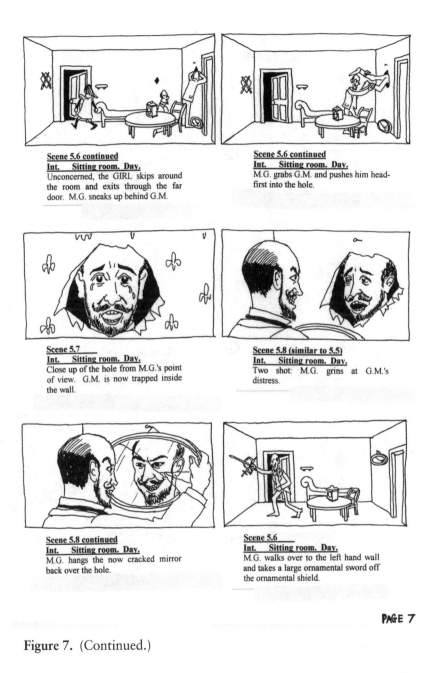

Scene 5.6 continued
Int.   Sitting room. Day.
Unconcerned, the GIRL skips around the room and exits through the far door. M.G. sneaks up behind G.M.

Scene 5.6 continued
Int.   Sitting room. Day.
M.G. grabs G.M. and pushes him head-first into the hole.

Scene 5.7
Int.   Sitting room. Day.
Close up of the hole from M.G.'s point of view. G.M. is now trapped inside the wall.

Scene 5.8 (similar to 5.5)
Int.   Sitting room. Day.
Two shot: M.G. grins at G.M.'s distress.

Scene 5.8 continued
Int.   Sitting room. Day.
M.G. hangs the now cracked mirror back over the hole.

Scene 5.6
Int.   Sitting room. Day.
M.G. walks over to the left hand wall and takes a large ornamental sword off the ornamental shield.

PAGE 7

Figure 7. (Continued.)

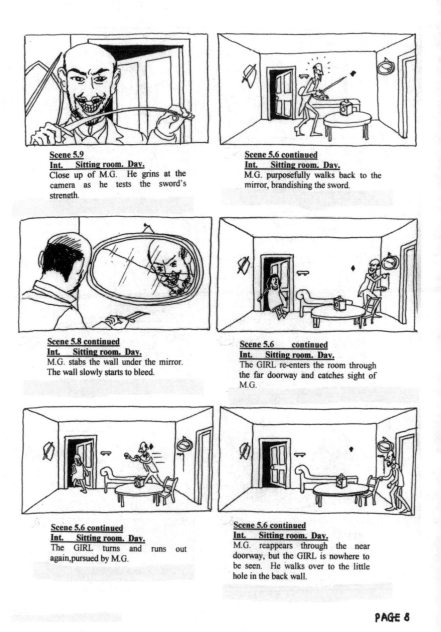

Scene 5.9
Int.   Sitting room. Day.
Close up of M.G. He grins at the camera as he tests the sword's strength.

Scene 5.6 continued
Int.   Sitting room. Day.
M.G. purposefully walks back to the mirror, brandishing the sword.

Scene 5.8 continued
Int.   Sitting room. Day.
M.G. stabs the wall under the mirror. The wall slowly starts to bleed.

Scene 5.6   continued
Int.   Sitting room. Day.
The GIRL re-enters the room through the far doorway and catches sight of M.G.

Scene 5.6 continued
Int.   Sitting room. Day.
The GIRL turns and runs out again, pursued by M.G.

Scene 5.6 continued
Int.   Sitting room. Day.
M.G. reappears through the near doorway, but the GIRL is nowhere to be seen. He walks over to the little hole in the back wall.

PAGE 8

Figure 7. (Continued.)

122

Scene 5.9
Int.   Sitting room. Day.
Close up of M.G. and the little hole:
M.G. looks at the hole and then grins
at the camera. He has had an idea.

Scene 5.6 (as 1.1) cont'd.
Int.   Sitting room. Day.
It is some time later. Cautiously the
GIRL re-enters the room through the
far doorway. Seeing that the coast is
clear she runs back to the little hole.

Scene 5.10
Int.   Sitting room. Day.
Close up of the hole: the GIRL jumps
into the hole.

Scene 6.1
Int.   Inside wall.   Day.
Ultra close-up of M.G.'s teeth.   Very
quick zoom in as his jaws chomp shut.

Scene 6.2
Int.   Inside wall.   Day.
Wider shot of M.G. inside the wall.
He grins at the camera and wipes his
mouth: he has eaten the GIRL!

Scene 7.1   (as1.1)
Int.   Sitting room. Day.
All is quiet in the sitting room once
more.

PAGE 9

Figure 7. (Continued.)

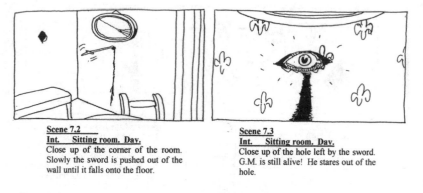

Scene 7.2
Int.   Sitting room. Day.
Close up of the corner of the room.
Slowly the sword is pushed out of the
wall until it falls onto the floor.

Scene 7.3
Int.   Sitting room. Day.
Close up of the hole left by the sword.
G.M. is still alive! He stares out of the
hole.

Scene 7.1 continued
Int.   Sitting room. Day.
G.M.'s HOUSEKEEPER enters the
room.

Scene 7.4
Int.   Sitting room. Day.
Close up of the HOUSEKEEPER
looking around the room.

Scene 7.5
Int.   Sitting room. Day.
The HOUSEKEEPER sits on the
chaise longue and notices the clock
sitting on the table.

Scene 8.1
Int.   Inside wall. Day.
Close up of G.M. trapped inside the
wall in distress. He tries to call out to
the HOUSEKEEPER.

PAGE 10

Scene 9.1
Int.   Sitting room. Day.
Close up of the hole with G.M.'s eye
looking through it. He starts to cry.

Scene 10.1
Int.   Inside wall. Day.
G.M.'s point of view through the hole:
the HOUSEKEEPER puts the clock
back on the wall and leaves the room.

Scene 10.2 (as 8.1)
Int.   Inside wall. Day.
Close up of G.M. in despair.

Scene 11.1 (as1.1)
Int.   Sitting room. Day.
The sitting room is silent once more.

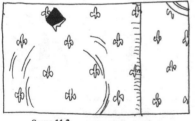

Scene 11.2
Int.   Sitting room. Day.
Close up of the small hole in the back
wall. Below the hole the wallpaper
starts to bulge.

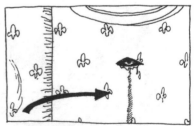

Scene 11.2 continued
Int.   Sitting room. Day.
As the wallpaper starts to bulge the
camera pans round to the right hand
wall and the hole below the mirror.

PAGE II

125

Scene 11.3
Int.   Sitting room. Day.
Close up of the hole below the mirror.
We can see G.M.'s downcast eye. A
shadow falls across the wall.

Scene 11.4
Int.   Sitting room. Day.
Close up of a gruesome knife cutting
through the wallpaper.

Scene 11.5
Int.   Sitting room. Day.
Close up of G.M.'s face appearing
through the slit in the wallpaper.

Scene 11.6
Int.   Sitting room. Day.
Two shot of G.M. and his saviour.

Scene 11.7
Int.   Sitting room. Day.
Two shot from a low angle. It is the
GIRL! She has escaped and has come
back for him.

Scene 11.8 (as 1.1)
Int.   Sitting room. Day.
The GIRL helps G.M. to his feet.

PAGE 12

Scene 11.9
Int.   Sitting room. Day.
Two shot of the GIRL and G.M.. G.M.
sees a huge hole in the back wall.
Obviously the girl cut herself out of
M.G. and also cut her way out of the
wall.

Scene 11.10
Int.   Sitting room. Day.
Close up of the GIRL's face from
G.M.'s point of view. She smiles.

Scene 11.8
Int.   Sitting room. Day.
The clock on the back wall strikes
twelve. They look round at it.

Scene 11.11
Int.   Sitting room. Day.
Close up of the clock: it is working
again.

Scene 11.12
Int.   Sitting room. Day.
Tight close up of the GIRL and G.M.
They kiss

Scene 11.12 continued
Int.   Sitting room. Day.
The film frame contracts to a circle
which contracts until we can only see
their lips. Fade to black.

The End.

PAGE 13

© MARTIN PICKLES 1999

G.M.

Script/summary by Martin Pickles

Please note: the film has no dialogue so this is
merely a list of stage directions

INT. EDWARDIAN SITTING ROOM. DAY.

A man ('G.M.') sits at a table reading his corre-
spondence. The remains of a light lunch sit in
front of him.

His HOUSEKEEPER enters the room and walks over to
pick up his breakfast tray. They exchange pleasan-
tries, after which she leaves the room.

G.M. gets up for a pace around. The clock on the
back wall stops ticking with a clunk. G.M. compares the time on the clock - two minutes to
twelve - with his pocket watch, which reads ten
past one. He goes over to the clock takes it down
off the wall very carefully and puts it on the
table. He turns back to the wall to get the
clock's key and finds, where the clock was
hanging, a hole in the wallpaper (hole 1) through
which a human eye is looking out. G.M. does a
shocked double take and then turns back to the
wall: the eye has gone and the hole is empty.

G.M. looks into the hole.

G.M. sticks his fingers in the hole: it moves
slightly along the wall. He continues and pushes
it right the way across the wall and eventually it
passes the face of a GIRL inside the wall. She has
a serene expression with both eyes closed.

G.M. looks on in amazement. The Girl's face disappears as a shadow covers her.

G.M. tears at the hole (hole 2) until it becomes
large and tattered. Inside the wall is an array of
figures draped across each other, wearing the
clothes of decades earlier. They all have their
eyes closed and move only slightly, like figures
in their sleep. The sides of the hole grow back
slowly until the hole is as small as it was to
begin with.

G.M. turns away in shock and flops onto the
chaise-longue. He thinks for a moment and notices
the mirror on the right-hand wall. He looks from
the mirror to hole 2 on the back wall and gets up,
walks over to the mirror and takes it off the
wall.

G.M. takes the mirror off the right-hand wall and
reveals a much larger hole (hole 3) through which
an evil version of his own face: 'M.G.', stares
back at him. The surprise makes G.M. drop the
mirror which lands at his feet and breaks. He
looks down at the mirror, which nearly hit his
toes, and as he does so M.G. shoots out of hole 3.
By the time G.M. looks back at the hole, it is
empty. G.M. sticks his head into the hole. Unknown
to him M.G. is hiding behind the table behind him.

As G.M. stares into hole 3 the Girl appears out of
hole 2. She skips around the room, unconcerned by
her surroundings and then exits via the left-hand
door.

M.G. rushes G.M. from behind and pushes him into
hole 3. He grins triumphantly at the imprisoned
G.M. and places the mirror back over the hole.

M.G. prances across the room to the left-hand wall
and takes down a small ornamental sword. He tests

its strength and shoots a grin at the camera. He walks back to the right-hand wall where G.M. is trapped, brandishing the sword as he goes. He carefully pushes the sword into the wall just under the mirror.

As he does so the Girl re-enters the room via the left-hand door. The sight of M.G. stabbing the wall brings her out of her thoughts and she stares at him in terror before turning on her heel and running out of the room. M.G. chases after her through the left-hand door. A moment later he reappears through the right-hand door. The Girl is nowhere to be seen.

M.G. thinks for a minute. He looks over at hole 2 and grins at the camera.

Some time later: the Girl re-enters the room through the left hand door. She finds the room empty but looks around cautiously. She goes over to the left-hand wall and takes down the remaining ornamental sword which she secretes in her dress. She runs towards hole 2 in the back wall and jumps into it.

As she does so, inside the wall M.G.'s jaws slam shut, devouring her. He wipes his mouth gleefully.

Outside the room is quiet once more. The sword which is still stuck in the wall under the mirror is slowly pushed out and drops out onto the floor. G.M.'s eye appears at the hole. Inside the wall we see him alive but in considerable distress.

Hearing the sound of the sword, the Housekeeper re-enters the room calling for G.M. Surprised that the room is empty she looks around and sits for a moment on the chaise longue. She gets up to go out, notices the clock on the table as she passes it and puts it back on the wall. She exits.

Inside the wall G.M. sees her so near to him, yet oblivious to his cries. As she leaves he sinks into despair. The room is empty once more.

The clock on the back wall starts to tick again. The paper on the back wall becomes stained with blood.

Over on the right-hand wall we can see the hole and G.M.'s downcast eye. A shadow falls across the wall. A blade starts to cut upwards through the paper below the mirror. G.M. is revealed through the expanding gash in the wall paper. He looks up at his saviour: it is the Girl, holding an ornamental sword.

She holds out her hand and helps him to his feet. Serenely he follows her into the room. He looks around at the back wall: it has a huge bloody gash in it and the deflated remains of M.G. lie in a pool of blood on the floor. The Girl smiles at G.M. who smiles back, unconcerned, even amused, by the gory scene.

The clock strikes twelve. G.M. and the Girl look at the clock and each other and laugh. They kiss.

Notes

1. Martin Pickles, script notes.
2. The quotations in this chapter from Martin Pickles are from an interview with the author.

Chapter 8

Room Eleven

Room Eleven is a fifteen-minute film written by Eoin O'Callaghan, directed by Clive Brill and produced by Tom Treadwell and Maureen Murray. The full script appears at the end of this chapter.

>> **R**oom *Eleven* is a horror pastiche where the slaughter of an innocent child may or may not have occurred and the Hitchcockian twist provides the essential intake of breath that comes with the unsettling ending. Here the dead return, not as zombies revived by radiation, as in George Romero's low-budget *Night of the Living Dead*, but as an obsessive memory that moves as if by osmosis between the minds of the principal characters.

At fifteen minutes, the film breaks the ten-and-under barrier self-imposed by producers faced with the usual twins of evil: cash constraints and an eye for the bite-sized time slots in typical festival and broadcasting schedules.

These considerations were secondary in green-lighting *Room Eleven*. Pacificus Productions was in the process of developing a horror script with Clive Brill attached to direct and needed to show potential backers that their established radio, TV and theater director could leap the gap to a feature.

The production company dropped £30,000 in the kitty and engaged Maureen Murray to make it happen. After ten years working with *enfant terrible* Ken Russell and another ten as an independent producer, Maureen had the web of friends and favors needed to bring in a crew of experienced technicians, hire the equipment, catering, make-up and wardrobe, and shoot in five days a short film with the feeling and style of a feature. Impossible?

'It's like skiing blindfold. I wouldn't recommend it, but yes, it's possible.'[1]

Maureen began where the process always begins: with the script. Working closely with writer Eoin O'Callaghan, she helped trim out the fat and encouraged the writer to ensure that every word and gesture carried its weight. 'Writers often resist this, their darlings cast into the abyss, but when the job's done and you read through the new draft – it always reads better.'

With the script more sharply in focus, director Clive Brill had to be convinced that the very scene he cherished most, where one of the characters throws herself out of a window, needed a hard cut from her climbing up on the sill to the body lying spreadeagled on the ground below, just as dramatic, if less spectacular, and a whole lot of saving in terms of time: the most expensive commodity on set. On a feature, it is normal to get about 2½ minutes of cut and finished film a day. On *Room Eleven*, they were aiming to get at least three minutes a day and still maintain feature quality.

Another crucial decision was to hire Roger Tooley and his Steadicam for a day. This 80 lb piece of equipment that straps on to a body harness, and looks a lot like a military flame thrower, can chase through gardens and upstairs, as ghosts are wont to do, and avoids rolling the DOP over miles of track on a dolly. Garrett Brown had developed the gyro-stabilized camera for the film industry and, when Stanley Kubrick tried it out in 1977, he discovered that the operator could 'walk, run and climb stairs while retaining a rock-steady image.'[2]

Kubrick had just purchased Childwick Bury, a remote manor house in rural Hertfordshire, and tested both the camera and its inventor to their limits on *The Shining*: the story of a man coping with writer's block. Kubrick wanted the Steadicam to do things it had never done before and Brown was employed to make it possible. 'I realized by the afternoon of the first day's work,' Brown was to observe phlegmatically, "that here was a whole new ball game, and that the word *reasonable* was not in Kubrick's lexicon.'[3]

It is probably why Kubrick's films remain memorable and why the camera movements envisaged for *Room Eleven* were inspired by *The Shining*.

Like all good ghost stories, the script required a gothic mansion with turrets, towers and macabre gargoyles for intermittent close-ups and reaction shots, not cliché but *de rigueur* for the genre. First AD Simon Hinkley had become attached to the project and he knew just the place: Chenies Manor House, a Tudor pile that began life as a settlement mentioned in the Domesday survey of 1086 and where, according to the house history brochure, 'the sepulchral footsteps of a lame man are occasionally heard on the staircase . . .' The lame man is said to be Henry VIII, who visited the house with Katherine Howard, the fifth Queen; she was having an affair with royal aide Thomas Culpepper at the time, so haunting footsteps are hardly surprising.

Chenies is open to the public from spring until autumn and the present owner, Elizabeth MacLeod Matthews, agreed to allow the house to be used for the shoot with a generosity that extended to her taking part as an extra in the dining scene. I do not know who suggested this, but can safely assume it was Maureen Murray, who knew I was writing this book and called suggesting that I fill another of the vacant seats at the table.

With the cast, extras and crew in place, Maureen began calling hire facilities for equipment and film stock. There had been a surge of projects greenlit at the same time, but having brought in the bucks on numerous features, Maureen used her long-standing contacts to acquire everything needed for the five-day shoot at about a quarter of book price. 'You always have to bargain with the hire companies. No one pays list price and, with a short film, they tend to be generous,' she adds. 'There was the usual Friday frenzy and everything finally arrived at the last minute.'

I was able to observe how the budget is stretched from my point of view as an extra, and discovered that the crew were working that week for nothing, or next to nothing, for many diverse and complicated reasons: a gaffer wants to partner with a particular DOP; a third AD gets the chance to be a second; assistants in set design, wardrobe and make-up graduate to heads of department; camera loaders and focus pullers exchange jobs, assist the sound man by holding the boom, or the props department by sticking something on to something. The film set is hierarchical, the master in each department taking on acolytes much like teachers in Eastern philosophy and training them to one day replace them.

On a short film, everyone pitches in, scurrying around with determined expressions and silver wheels of gaffer tape hanging from their belts. There are two things that hold the film industry together: gaffer tape and networking, who you know – as in most fields – as important as what you know, the result being an odd blend of the egalitarian and nepotistic. On *Room Eleven* when we broke for lunch, Tom Treadwell queued up in the biting cold for his chicken green curry and rice, the same as everyone else.

Another reason for taking on a short film is that top technicians use the opportunity to experiment. 'It's like going back to film school and being tested,' says DOP Philip Robertson. 'You don't have this lens or that piece of equipment – so what are you going to do about it? And what you do is make do. It's good not to become too spoilt. On a short film resources are scarce so you have to stretch yourself and make things work.'

The DOP has an assistant, loader and operator, each with their own vital functions and serving the long apprenticeship that leads to becoming a director of photography. The DOP will often be asked to choose the lighting chief and head of props – the gaffer and grip – because the producer knows that when people have worked together before, like formation dancers, they have learned how to move in harmony.

A producer or director will often contact a DOP because they admire the lighting and camera work on a particular film. It should not be forgotten that, experimentation aside, with *Room Eleven* being shot with high production values, the crew and cast would have at the end of the week a further credit, a valuable showreel and an extended loop on their web of industry contacts.

Philip Robertson had long ago learned that some directors want you 'to light up and shut up.' Others, he adds, want a little bit more, and his calm presence on set was ideal for Brill's début. They discussed shots and tried alternatives, listened to suggestions from first AD Hinkley, and bowed always to Brill's final decision. Glenda Jackson once said in a *Guardian* interview at the National Film Theatre that a good director listens to everyone – 'unlike a politician.' Nonetheless, it's an unwritten law: the director's always right, even when he's wrong.

Roger Tooley puts it another way. 'With inexperienced directors you are walking a tightrope. Some are arrogant, but most ask: what do you think? And when they do, you can insert your own artistic vision, which is what it's all about.' He adds: 'As a cameraman, you have to extract the shot the director wants and, if they are new to the game, you have to understand what it is they are trying to achieve when they don't actually know how to achieve it.'

It is the independence of operating his own Steadicam that attracts Tooley, but the real world for a cinematographer he sees is in 'the green eye of an Arri 35mm camera,' and that's the work he prefers. He describes the film business as an addiction worse than any drug. Once you start, you can't stop. He spent two months working on a French film set in the desert. There were sand storms on a daily basis, the hours were long, he hated every minute he was there and looked back with nostalgia at the moment the plane touched down back at Heathrow.

'You would think that a big budget film would be more organized, but that's not the case,' says Tooley. 'On a short film you have to be organized, and after the intensity of working on a feature, there's nothing like the close atmosphere and the sense of working as a team you get on a short.'

I had joined the team a few days before on a rainy bleak Wednesday when Maedhbh McMahon arrived like a glimpse of sunshine with sparkling eyes, a shooting script under her arm and a camera in her bag. A quick kiss on the cheek and she was bounding upstairs to poke around in my wardrobe. She pulled out various shirts and decided on pale blue, some fawn cargo pants, brown docksiders and a light jacket with a faint check. She uhmed and aghed over the jacket and took some photo stills to show the director. My big scene was being shot in a room rich in patterns, so the cast were being dressed in solid colors.

As the costume designer, Maedhbh (pronounced Maeve) had been poking into quite a few wardrobes during the hectic days prior to shooting. She had worn her heels flat walking around Camden Market and had popped into the National Theatre's warehouse in Brixton in search of a 1960s outfit to be used in the flashback sequence. Renting from hire houses isn't cheap, anything from £60 per week per costume, but the National does special deals for budget filmmakers.

Maedhbh starts out by breaking down the script in order to relate the costumes to the characters and figures out what costumes are going to be needed for each day's shooting. As films are not shot chronologically, all the costumes have to be ready in case the shooting schedule changes. Sometimes, the director may decide a character doesn't look right in a certain color, it throws out the entire design, 'and everyone,' says Maedhbh, 'ends up running around like headless chickens.'

When the budget permits, the costume designer will need at least two sets of clothes for each character, but even that is rarely sufficient. If a scene is shot in pouring rain, a dry jacket becomes wet, and while the actor wears the spare costume for the second take, the wardrobe department is anxiously drying everything with a hair dryer ready for the third. If a scene requires characters wading through mud, the problem is easy to imagine, more 'headless chickens.'

And then there's the nightmare of squibbing – the explosion of bloody patches when characters are shot – and, of course, it looks far better on a nice crisp white shirt. In gangster movies and war films, the costume department spends all night in the laundry like a clean up party for the mafia.

Are there any tricks to the trade?

Maedhbh McMahon would only give away two: new clothes are soaked in cold tea to take out the stiffness and age them; and by the end of a film, costumes are held together by safety pins and gaffer tape. 'What the eye can't see, the director's not going to worry about.'

Maedhbh began her career after studying art history and spent five years working as a milliner. She helped make props as an assistant on *Captain Corelli's Mandolin*, the big-budget Nick Cage/Penelope Cruz feature shot in Greece, and moved straight on to making hats for the extras in the *Harry Potter* films. 'To become a costume designer it is important to make contacts,' she said. 'I was lucky because there were seven different designers working on *Captain Corelli*. When I returned to London, they were all preparing different films and I was offered work straight away.'

Even though she now has wide experience on features and TV drama, Maedhbh enjoys the intimacy of short films. 'The atmosphere is always very friendly,' she says, echoing Roger Tooley, "and you get this nice feeling that you are working as a team.'

The following day I received a four-page fax from production manager Sam Holt with directions to Chenies, a map and final instructions: wear warm clothes. I understood why as we approached the house. Horses were galloping through the low-lying mist clinging to the fields and the brick chimneys and towers had the look of enormous props below the leaded vault of the sky. It only needed a flash of lightning and we would have been in a Dracula movie. I was brought down to earth by the piquant, early hour smell of frying bacon.

It had just gone seven and the caterers were serving robust portions of egg, bacon, sausages, hash brown potatoes and beans. 'Heart attack on a plate,' said the first AD, leading me from the cold courtyard with my laden dish into the dining room where there were urns of coffee, boxes of cereal and plates of Danish pastries. It was Tuesday. The crew had worked a solid twelve hours the previous day and was stoking up for the day ahead. Like an army going into battle, a film crew marches on its stomach. In fact, as Simon Hinkley pointed out, when the film business was reviving after the last war, a large number of sergeant majors joined the profession as first assistant directors.

It was easy to see why as Hinkley managed the schedule, barking out orders to the crew, protecting his officers – the director and DOP – while they considered performance and the visual realization of Eoin O'Callaghan's script.

The first AD's role is to ensure that the director's vision is accomplished with the minimum of fuss or delay. He will make sure the extras are ready when they are needed; he'll tell make-up to bring a shawl for the scantily clad actress to keep warm between takes. If a horse is going to be sent galloping across the misty fields, he'll be behind the groom making sure the beast is saddled and biting at the bit. A good first AD – and that's why Simon Hinkley was brought into *Room Eleven* – will see problems before they happen, and stop them happening. It is up to him, finally, to see that the director gets through his day's schedule and is prepared for the next day. In this respect, the AD also has one eye on the money; if a film does fall behind, he's likely to get the blame.

After the first AD has ensured everyone is ready for a take, on set he directs the extras and controls crowd scenes. While the director is concentrating on his leading players, the first AD must capture the same vision from the rest of the cast and, in this way, the assistant director is in training for that day when (and if) he wants to move up the greasy pole. The first AD is assisted by a second AD, who runs around on the first's instructions and fills out the production reports with the aid of the script supervisor's notes. The first AD needs eyes in the back of his head: the second AD is that pair of eyes.

After breakfast, I watched Roger Tooley strapped into his Steadicam running through the drifting mist among the pruned rose bushes in the garden, capturing the movements of the unseen poltergeist. Andrew Ellis, another extra, had turned up with a camera and was quietly wandering around the set taking photo stills. Sisters Helena and Lottie Rice, two more extras, were wisely using the day they had skived off school to do some exam revision. An extra's day is long and, if directing is death by a thousand questions, playing bit-parts is death from waiting.

It was almost noon when Simon Hinkley finally rounded us up, rushed us through make-up and readied Andrew Ellis, Helena, Lottie and myself for the dining scene. The skyscraper-tall producer Tom Treadwell sat at the head of the table and Elizabeth MacLeod Matthews appeared from the warren of rooms at Chenies to join us.

We sat sipping apple juice from crystal glasses and imagined – with little success on my part – that it was Chardonnay, and invented *polite* conversation as we waited for Avril King, our host. We turned *with courteous interest* on hearing her voice, but the moment she entered, she was hurrying out again, distressed by the vision seen by her, though not we extras. We now looked suitably astonished – so astonished, in fact, Clive Brill called a quick cut and we did it all again, with slightly less awe.

The scene was repeated several times until Clive and DOP Philip Robertson both nodded judiciously, a quiet understanding reached between them, and the process was repeated with Celia Barry floating through the dining room, a ghostly presence all in white, unseen by us, but terrifying for Avril King.

We controlled our gasps, looked surprised rather than shocked and, in little more than an hour the two twenty-second scenes were in the can. While the grips started dismantling the kit, we followed the smell of curry out to the parking lot and stamped our feet as we queued before the catering van. It was lunch time. I was starving, a big breakfast always does that, and I sat down with Maureen Murray curious as to why she was producing a short film, her first, after being involved in various capacities with more than twenty features.

'I wanted to work with the writer and director,' she answered without hesitation. 'Eoin O'Callaghan and Clive Brill have a strong synergy between them and this was an opportunity to see them in action. Often you are invited to work on a project that has already started, it's like a moving train. This one was waiting at the station.' She continued, warming into the metaphor: 'Often, the rails have already been laid and you know the train's going to derail before it gets to the next station. On *Room Eleven* I had the chance to get in at the beginning and set the film up properly. Keep it on track.'

For Maureen, the most important aspect of a short film is preparation. The producer must ask two key questions at the outset: why are we making this film? And what is the market for it? If both questions can be answered positively, it is then essential not to compromise when it comes to finding crew, hiring equipment and casting experienced players, in this case the well-known actors Anton Lasser, who plays the psychiatrist, Susan Brown, as Avril King, and Poppy Miller in the dual roles as Sophie Calder and Celia Barry.

'Making a short film shouldn't be really that different from making a feature. You need to keep everyone involved, from the runner to the star, and set up a thoroughly professional level of production.'

A sympathetic and flexible editor was needed to allow Clive to immerse himself in the editing experience. Maureen signed up Xavier Russell, who has both the quick turnaround flare fundamental to television and the more measured proficiency brought into 35mm features. Even from rough cut to fine cut, a few nips and tucks were required, and Xavier she knew had the artistic and technical skills, as well as understanding how to achieve the pace and character development visualized by the director.

Clive was completing the process when I called to ask him about his experience directing *Room Eleven*. This was his response:

The first thing that hits a new director is the sheer number of aspects of the film he has to take responsibility for whilst simultaneously respecting the art of those he has chosen to work with. Actors will give you a whole range of performances you hadn't necessarily thought of; learning how to shape, accept and sometimes reject what they have to offer is key. But from the script up - everyone and everything is offering you an almost bewildering range of choices. The budgets on short films are tight, so you simply don't have the luxury (as in say theater or radio) of trying quite a few things out before committing to a decision. It suddenly hits home that decision-making – from placement of props to choice of wigs, to placement of camera to interpretation of lines, all require a rapid and committed response.

Looking at the rushes, I can see all the places where I allowed my judgment to be slightly compromised by being focused on something else I thought more important. Watching a scene unfold on a monitor requires a hundred eyes. How's the frame? How was the move? Does the color of the picture behind draw the eye away from the actor? Is the camera moving in a way that organically compliments the scene? Above all: are you telling the story, and making the audience understand the way you want them to?

It is impossible to say how closely the finished product resembles the initial picture in your mind. The dreams I had before I started shooting were a mixture of interpretation of script – other film moments I had seen – and knowledge of what I thought the actors and key crew might bring to the set. But inevitably nothing is quite as envisioned. A new, fresh, sometimes alarming perspective is flickering before me.

The editing process is like a new buzz of electricity after the film is exposed. All this mass of material sometimes appears limiting. But the joy of working with a new pair of eyes – and amazing Avid technology – suddenly gives you myriad choices you hardly dared suspect were there. More choices equals more decision-making of course . . .

I had always known starting at the beginning of my career in radio that sound played a hugely significant role in film-making. I mean, the combination of fx, speech and music. A few days before the final dub we have a locked off picture, with luck the best performances and the most imaginatively edited version of the material we shot. And yet – the music's not on, the well-placed shot door is unheard – even the speech is woolly. I won't know if the film's any good until the final sound effects are added. And I feel instinctively that, without sound, the pictures will never completely work. I think like all directors I wish I'd had four times the shooting time I was given. To me, every scene shouts a missed camera angle, a lost CU, a slight mis-emphasis, a head turned a fraction too far. I pray the audience doesn't notice.

The whole experience has confirmed to me what I always suspected. With all the frustration of never being completely in control of everything – of always feeling that the picture might slip away from one's grasp – of hoping that the art at the end will justify the process of getting there – it's the most exhilarating job on the planet.

ROOM ELEVEN

Screenplay by Eoin O'Callaghan

Directed by Clive Brill

Produced by Tom Treadwell and Maureen Murray

1 EXT. MAYFIELD HOUSE, ENTRANCE AND GRAVEL PATHWAY. EVE.

Immense pillars topped with stone cherubs support a distinctive wrought iron gate, leading onto A GRAVEL DRIVEWAY. We follow the driveway around to the right.

C/U of CHERUB.

2 EXT. MAYFIELD HOUSE, ENTRANCE AND GRAVEL PATHWAY. EVE.

A GATE leading onto the garden. Through this we discover a second GATE - which leads us past the nursery garden and which sweeps up to a gloomy TUDOR PILE with hooded eaves and heavy with ivy. It is forbidding and uninviting - a Mervyn Peake drawing.

The front door creaks open and yields to black. O/S we hear a baby's insistent CRYING.

C/U of CHERUB.

3 INT. MAYFIELD HOUSE. EVE.

We travel along a corridor and into the main reception area. This in turn leads onto an ante room and then a dining room. 5 GUESTS are seated for dinner. We pass them and swing hard right into a corridor, past a sitting room with another guest, and up a spiral staircase. Establish: photos of boy and girl and yellow cross on window of the stairwell.

Now onto the upper floors. Panelled corridors lead
left and right. We head to the left past the tapestry
room. The crying MORE SHRILL now - Straight ahead is
ROOM 11 - an ornate bedroom. We enter. In the corner
of the room a small wooden door stands ajar.

C/U of CHERUB.

4 INT. ANTE ROOM AND ARMOURY. EVE.

We follow the source of the crying up some stairs.

Through a small ante room to a long wooden corridor:
the armoury. Through the gloom at the end we pick up
SOPHIE CALDER, 30s, by a window - her face bleak and
tear strewn. A bottle of TRANQUILLISERS lies half
spilled on the table at which she is seated. In another
corner is a CRIB. The baby's crying is now unbearable.

ANGLE ON the anguished face of Sophie as she hauls
herself to her feet. She almost sleepwalks to the crib.

She takes THE PILLOW from the cot and without emotion
places it over the baby's mewling mouth.

HEART THUMPING exertion fills Sophie's face as she
presses downwards.

At last THE NOISE CEASES. There is a moment of absolute
calm.

Sophie walks to the window and presses her hands against
it.

5 EXT. MAYFIELD HOUSE. EVE.

PU SHOT FROM EXT BELOW

Sophie pressing against the window. Is she going to jump?

6 INT. ARMOURY. EVE.

ANGLE ON Sophie as she turns back to face the room and catches sight of herself in the mirror beside the crib.

The mirror smashes in a tremendous explosion of sound.

7 INT. ARMOURY. EVE.

POV from the window.

Sophie's broken body on the gravel below.

8 EXT. HOUSE. EVE.

POV the ground.

Sophie's broken body.

9 INT. HARLEY ST. OFFICE OF THERAPIST PAUL LAVELLE, 47. DAY.

Sophie sits opposite LAVELLE in a leather chair. She looks stricken.

Lavelle is lean and intellectual, a man born to listen.

>   **LAVELLE**
> And?

>   **SOPHIE**
>   (*nonplussed*))
> That's it. That's all there is.

>   **LAVELLE**
> Do you think you killed the baby?

>   **SOPHIE**
> Yes. Of course.

>   **LAVELLE**
>   (*pressing her*)
> And why do you think you did that?

Silence.

>   **LAVELLE (CONT'D)**
> Might it have something to do
> with the termination?

>   **SOPHIE**
>   (*Losing patience*)
> Look, I know *why* I keep having
> this dream. I just want it to stop.

Lavelle picks up Sophie's file.

>   **LAVELLE**
> When did you last have a holiday
> - I mean a complete break from
> work?

>   **SOPHIE**
> I haven't the time.

>   **LAVELLE**
> Don't you and - er . . . Danny get
> out of London occasionally?

> SOPHIE
> Danny's not around any more . . .

Silence.

> LAVELLE
> If I were to recommend a quiet
> country house, where you could
> take time alone, read a few
> books, walk in the fields, what
> would you say?

> SOPHIE
> I'd be bored out of my brain.

Lavelle sighs.

> LAVELLE
> Let some air at the wound,
> Sophie. Make some space. Will you
> at least think about it?

He hands her a card with the legend:

Mayfield House – Country House Retreat. Prop:
Avril King.

> SOPHIE
> Is this one of those Harley
> Street scams where the analysts
> get a percentage on referrals?

> LAVELLE
> You've been working in the media
> too long.

He rises and she takes the card.

> SOPHIE
> I'll think about it.

As the door closes behind her, Lavelle experiences a flash image of SOPHIE SMOTHERING A CHILD.

RESUME SCENE 2

Shocked at the vividness of this image, he sits back in his chair and shuts his eyes.

FADE OUT.

10 EXT. THE A1. SOPHIE'S CAR. DAY.

Up and past. She passes a sign for The North.

11 INT. SOPHIE'S CAR. DAY

ANGLE ON Sophie driving intently. The rain beats down on the windscreen.

She punches out Lavelle's number on her hands-free mobile.

12 INT. LAVELLE'S OFFICE. DAY.

Lavelle's phone buzzes and he picks it up.

> **LAVELLE**
> Hello. Paul Lavelle.

13 INT. SOPHIE'S CAR / LAVELLE'S OFFICE. DAY.

WE CUT BETWEEN THE TWO:

> **SOPHIE**
> (*Jokily*)
> Hi. I wanted you to know I'm on
> my way to your 'country house
> retreat'.

> **LAVELLE (O.S.)**
> Hey. Good for you.

> **SOPHIE**
> It's not a health farm, is it?

> **LAVELLE**
> God, no. Guaranteed heart attack
> on a plate.

> **SOPHIE**
> Great, soon I'll be clinically
> depressed *and* overweight.

> **LAVELLE (O.S.)**
> You are not clinically depressed.

> **SOPHIE**
> (*sarcastic*)
> Right, I forgot. I'm just having bad
> dreams . . .

> **LAVELLE**
> Sophie. Stop it. Relax. I'll talk
> to you next week.

She ends the call and drives on through the
lashing rain.

FLASHBACK TO SC. 1: As the windscreen wipers deal
with the rain, each wipe presents Sophie with a
quick succession of flashbacks to her dream:

ROOM 11, THE BABY, THE PILLOW PRESSING DOWN.

RESUME SC. 5: She shuts her eyes on these images.

The blast of an air horn makes Sophie suddenly open her eyes.

Rear View as Sophie veers dangerously.

Close-up as she regains control of the car and herself.

THE AIR-HORN CROSSES TO:

14 INT. LAVELLE'S OFFICE. DAY.

LAVELLE'S eyes open suddenly. Disconcerted, he gathers his notes on Sophie Calder and puts them in a drawer.

15 INT. SOPHIE'S CAR. EVE.

Sophie as she spots the stone cherubs atop the immense gate posts. The House's familiarity begins to register.

The rain has abated. The sun shimmers off the wet tarmac. Mayfield House looms imposingly.

16 INT. MAYFIELD HOUSE. EVE. POV FROM WINDOW.

Sophie's car is seen entering the driveway, the car makes its way round to the right of the house and towards the rear.

17 EXT. MAYFIELD HOUSE. EVE.

Sophie now on foot. A wooden door leads onto the garden. Through this we discover a second door – which leads past the nursery garden and which sweeps up to the great house.

By the time she reaches the front door it has dawned on Sophie that Mayfield House is, indeed, the house in her nightmare.

Her first instinct is to ring Lavelle again, but her cell phone has 'no service'.

A moment of apprehension. Then a decision to press on.

18 INT. MAYFIELD HOUSE. RECEPTION. EVE.

Sophie enters cautiously. She rings a BELL and studies the somehow familiar surroundings. She tries the bell again. She calls out.

> **SOPHIE**
> Mrs King.

There is movement in the office behind reception.
> **SOPHIE (CONT'D)**
> Sophie Calder. We spoke on the phone.

The proprietor, AVRIL KING, emerges cheerily from an office.
> **AVRIL**
> You made good time.

                    SOPHIE
      Yes, struck it lucky on the
      motorway.

Avril stops short - stunned when she sees Sophie's
face.

An awkward silence. The colour drains from Avril's
face.

                  SOPHIE (CONT'D)
        Mrs King. You alright?

Avril steadies herself without answering.

                  SOPHIE (CONT'D)
                 (pleasantly)
        Room 11? Isn't it?

Avril, struggles to regain her composure. She
reaches for a room key.

                    AVRIL
        Yes, that's right. Room 11.

                    SOPHIE
      Second floor.

How can she have known that? Avril regards her
with fear.

                    AVRIL
                 (abruptly)
        Dinner's at 8.30.

                    SOPHIE
                 (taken aback)
        Thank you.

Sophie lifts her case and heads for the stairs.
She drinks in the details of the house.

Avril watches her. Sophie appears to know exactly where she is going.

19 INT. MAYFIELD HOUSE. CORNER OF RECEPTION. EVE.

Avril shakily pours a long stiff drink. She is extremely agitated.

20 INT. MAYFIELD HOUSE. EVE.

As if by instinct, SOPHIE heads for ROOM 11 through the empty dining room.

21 INT. MAYFIELD HOUSE. STAIRWELL AND SECOND FLOOR CORRIDOR. EVE.

Sophie climbs the stairwell, passes though the tapestry room and reaches

THE DOOR OF ROOM 11.

She notices her hand is trembling. The door opens to reveal the room exactly as she had seen it in her dream. She goes rigid as if a blast of ice-cold air has taken her breath away. She proceeds cautiously into the room.

22 INT. MAYFIELD HOUSE. CORNER OF RECEPTION. EVE.

Avril draws hard on her cigarette. She catches sight of herself in a mirror in the corner of the reception. She is not pleased at her appearance.

Now suddenly beside her face in the mirror there appears the face of Sophie - or rather, someone very like Sophie. It is CELIA BARRY, (as we will discover) the previous owner of Mayfield House - now dead.

Celia - bleached hair and 1960s' dress - produces a lipstick and touches up her heavy carmine make-up. She dabs her lips then gazes resentfully at Avril.

The image disappears. Avril shudders, drains her drink in one and lifts the phone.

23 INT. LAVELLE'S OFFICE. EVE.

Lavelle sits quietly at his desk. The answer machine clicks on.

> ### AVRIL (O/S)
> (*sotto and full of anxiety*)
> Dr Lavelle. That woman you sent
> to me, Sophie Calder . . .

24 INT. RECEPTION MAYFIELD HOUSE. EVE.

> ### AVRIL
> It's Celia Barry - it's her to
> the life . . . . Please . . . Please call me
> as soon as possible

25 INT. LAVELLE'S OFFICE. EVE.

Lavelle regards the answer machine impassively.

26 EXT. SHOT OF MAYFIELD HOUSE. NIGHT.

Lights blazing.

27 INT. MAYFIELD HOUSE. ROOM 11. NIGHT.

Sophie sits at the dressing table. Every corner of the room is familiar to her. She turns and sees the wooden door ajar in the corner. She rises and moves towards it.

28 INT. MAYFIELD HOUSE. DINING ROOM. NIGHT.

Avril, dressed for the evening with considerably more make-up, greets the dinner guests. She is suddenly distracted.

We follow Avril's terrified line of vision and see the ghost of Celia Barry seated at the table, staring at her.

Avril is now oblivious to the guests. Her gaze is fixed on Celia, who heads for the second floor. Avril follows her.

29 INT. MAYFIELD HOUSE. THE ARMOURY. NIGHT.

Sophie moves along the long wooden corridor as in her dream towards an object she recognises with horror:

A CRIB in the corner.

It is as though she has lost the capacity to
breathe. A pain seers through her temple. She sits
unsteadily on a chair by a table.

Shakily, she pulls out a bottle of tranquillisers,
spilling them onto the table. She sits back in
terror and despair.

30 INT. MAYFIELD HOUSE. STAIRWELL AND SECOND FLOOR CORRIDOR. NIGHT.

Avril glimpses Celia through the stairwell window
and follows her.

Avril moves silently but briskly along the maze of
corridors. It is the same journey we travelled at
the very beginning of the film.

We hear a baby crying.

Avril momentarily freezes. But the baby's
insistent crying compels her forward towards ROOM
11. The baby's crying from inside the room is now
much louder.

Light spills through the half open door of Room
11. Avril pushes open the door and enters Room 11.

C/U of Stone Cherub.

31 INT. MAYFIELD HOUSE. THE ARMOURY. NIGHT.

Avril moves quickly through the wooden door up the
final steps towards the armoury.

As Avril enters. The crying suddenly stops.

Celia is removing an embroidered pillow from the crib where a baby now lies smothered. Sophie is nowhere to be seen.

ANGLE ON AVRIL: She looks in horror at the dead infant and screams.

> **AVRIL**
> Whose child is this? Whose child is this!

A movement attracts Avril's attention.

ANGLE ON The mirror by the crib, in which Avril sees Celia pressing her hands against the window panes - as if attempting to force her way through the glass.

C/U The Mirror. Suddenly the mirror shatters explosively.

Resume Sc 19: Instinctively Avril raises her arms to cover her head.

She whips round to look at the window. The window is intact. There is nothing there.

Avril rushes to the window and looks down.

Avril's POV: Celia lies broken on the driveway below.

32 EXT. MAYFIELD HOUSE. EVE.

ANGLE ON Celia's broken body on the driveway. POV the ground.

33 INT. MAYFIELD HOUSE. THE ARMOURY. NIGHT.

AVRIL reels back from the window shocked and appalled - but as she turns back into the room she has the second, more awful, surprise. There is:

Sophie sitting by the table looking at her, questioningly.

Avril holds her gaze. Neither is going to flinch.

As the camera pulls back we see both window and mirror intact.

34 INT. LAVELLE'S OFFICE. DAY.

SILENCE except for a ticking clock.

Avril turns to look at Lavelle's benign, all-comprehending face.

                    AVRIL
          You don't believe me.

Lavelle glances at a card for Mayfield House on the table between them.

                AVRIL (CONT'D)
          She was there.

                  LAVELLE
          I believe Sophie was there. Celia
          Barry died in 1964.

                    AVRIL
               (*definitely*)
          It was the same woman.

The clock ticks. Lavelle makes a note.

> **LAVELLE**
> Why did Celia Barry kill herself?

> **AVRIL**
> She'd murdered her child. She was
> driven to distraction, I presume.

Silence.

> **LAVELLE**
> Do you have many friends, Avril?

Avril shakes her head almost imperceptibly.

> **LAVELLE (CONT'D)**
> How much are you drinking at the
> moment?

Silence.

She sees him glance at the clock on his desk.

> **AVRIL**
> Is it time?

> **LAVELLE**
> Has Celia gone?

Avril considers this remark, then announces
simply.

> **AVRIL**
> I think she has.

Lavelle stands and ushers her to the door.

> **LAVELLE**
> Then you'll call me. If you need me.

She leaves and Lavelle shuts the door behind her.

FLASHBACK TO SC. 20 - in Lavelle's head - to the body of Celia lying dead on the driveway of Mayfield House, exactly as Avril described it earlier.

The image fades.

RESUME SC. 22: Lavelle breathes heavily and considers.

The telephone rings. He snatches it up.

> LAVELLE (CONT'D)
> Hello.

> SOPHIE (O.S.)
> You've heard, have you?

> LAVELLE
> (*non-committal*)
> Sophie. No. How was it?

35 INT. SOPHIE'S CAR / LAVELLE'S OFFICE. DAY.

WE CUT BETWEEN THE TWO:

> SOPHIE
> Avril King went berserk - burst into my room and attacked me - then had to be sedated. It was a nightmare. Has she got a drink problem?

Lavelle considers this version of events.

> **LAVELLE**
> God...

Just then Lavelle glances into an office mirror.
He sees a flash of Celia staring straight at him.

> **SOPHIE**
> And, that house - Mayfield House
> is the house in my dream. I mean
> like the same in every detail.
> I'm dreaming about the house of
> one of your patients. How do you
> explain that?

> **LAVELLE**
> (*distracted*)
> Lay-lines, crop circles -
> psychokinetic transference/

> **SOPHIE**
> (*emphatic*)
> I don't know what kind of voodoo
> you're at - it's very, very scary
> - but I haven't had the dream
> since I went there. Bizarre, eh?

Another flash of Celia in the mirror. Followed by:

FLASHBACK TO SC.19A. A flash of Celia's image
shattering in the mirror.

RESUME SC. 23: Lavelle cries out, involuntarily.

> **SOPHIE (CONT'D)**
> Dr Lavelle? What's happened?

Shaking and sweating, Lavelle places his back
against the wall, shuts his eyes tight.

> **SOPHIE (CONT'D)**
> Paul.

Another glance in the mirror. There is NOTHING there.

But sweat is running down Lavelle's face.

> **SOPHIE (CONT'D)**
> Paul. Answer me...

> **LAVELLE**
> Yeah.....Yes....It's ok. Yes.
> Look, I'm sorry ...I can't seem
> to...

> **SOPHIE (O.S.)**
> What's wrong?

Lavelle replaces the phone.

His hands are trembling. He wipes the sweat from his face with a handkerchief and breathes deeply. But:

In the mirror Lavelle sees images of Sophie Calder then Avril King, seated on his patient's couch. They stare at LAVELLE derisively from within his imagination. He breathes deeply. He begins to calm down. The images begin to fade.

The intercom sounds. The images evaporate. LAVELLE answers. It's his receptionist.

> **LAVELLE**
> Yes?

> **MARY (O.S.)**
> You know your last patient is
> here. It's ten past now.

> **LAVELLE**
> Just two minutes.

Lavelle goes to the mirror and peers in it. He glances back at the couch:

NOTHING.

He smooths his hair and presses the intercom.

> **LAVELLE (CONT'D)**
> OK, Mary.

> **MARY (O.S.)**
> She's on her way.

He takes a deep breath, dabs the sweat from his face with a handkerchief. We hear the door open.

> **CELIA (O.S.)**
> Paul?

A young woman in a 1960s' dress and bleached blond hair walks in. We just see her face. Lavelle's face freezes in terror. He is barely able to articulate her name.

> **LAVELLE**
> Celia?

> **CELIA**
> I've been having such dreadful nightmares.

The camera pulls back as Celia stretches out to Lavelle a tightly wrapped bundle - containing a child.

She smiles. Now she is his nightmare.

FADE OUT

Notes

1. The quotations in this chapter from Maureen Murray, Philip Robertson, Roger Tooley and Maedhbh McMahon are from interviews with the author.
2. Garrett Brown, in John Baxter, *Stanley Kubrick, A Biography* (Harper Collins, 1997)
3. Ibid.

Chapter 9

Greta May:
The Adaptation

Greta May is a 1,600 word short story first published in The Dream Zone. *It is in development with Metro 7 Underworld Films.*

>> Francis Ford Coppola with the three *Godfather* films became one of the most acclaimed film-makers of modern times. The scripts were adapted from Mario Puzo's books about the mafia, and what Coppola learned from the adaptation process was that where the writer has already labored over his narrative, the key elements of characterization and the story's major turning points are already in place.

With Hollywood film-makers always in competition to option the latest high-profile novel, Coppola in 1998 took the original step of launching *Zoetrope: All-Story*, a literary magazine that publishes innovative new fiction, and gives Coppola first rights to option the story for film. What Coppola had discovered was that in the neglected world of the short story there is a gold mine of precious material.

Short stories by their very nature contain no wasted words, every scene is vital; a good story has pace and rhythm, every gesture and nuance driving the narrative to a climax that is often both satisfying and unexpected: just what film-makers are looking for. If the short story writer has done his job well, the script won't exactly write itself, but the foundations are already in place.

It's a common complaint that the film is never like the book; more frequently, not as good as the book. But the forms do not bare comparison, and each must be as good as they can be within their own medium. The scriptwriter may decide to make the climax his opening scene and let the story unfold in retrospect. Perhaps he will see a story about twin brothers better told as one with twin sisters. The possibilities are limitless, but the elements are already there like cards to be reshuffled and dealt in endless new patterns.

As a short story, *Greta May* was written with the Eight-Point Guide in mind (see box on Page 18). When it came to adapting the story to an eight-minute script, the first draft remained true to the *literary* version, but on subsequent rewrites (scriptwriting is rewriting), with suggestions from producers Sacha Van Spall and Maureen Murray, the flashbacks and flash-forwards made much of the dialogue redundant and gave the story its visual form.

As a short film, *Greta May* is currently in pre-production with Metro 7 Underworld Films (info@metro7.com). At the same time, Sacha Van Spall is producing *Darwin's Theory*, with Cedric Behrel directing, and the same technicians working on both projects. 'These are two high-quality, high-profile, high-impact pieces of challenging and provocative cinema,' says Van Spall, "and they will be launched through an extensive promotion campaign led by a major PR company.'[1]

It will be a useful exercise for film-makers to study the short story below and make notes before reading the script. Decide how you would adapt the story, and compare it with my own adaptation. There is no right or wrong way to do this, but it will be interesting to see how I've done it, and how similar or dissimilar your own take on the story.

Greta May

She was glancing at the night's TV listings in the *Standard* when she became aware of the man staring at her. Studying her. It's something that just isn't done. Not on the tube. It's so intimate. While your body's rubbing against other bodies the last thing you want to do is make eye contact. She looked away. There was a movie with John Cusack, Channel 4, nine o'clock. Shame about the commercials. She'd microwave something during the breaks. Drink a glass of wine. Or two.

She glanced up. He was looking still. He smiled. Good teeth. She frowned. If she'd been in a pub she would have liked his brown eyes and broad shoulders. She looked down, then back up again, instinctively, as if against her will. He was writing something in a notebook. He tore out the page and gave it to her as the train slowed at Gloucester Road.

'My stop,' he said, and squeezed through the sliding doors before they closed.

His name was Richard. His number was 7376 7377. She wondered how he managed to get so many sevens. Was it lucky? For him? For her?

She screwed up the piece of paper and let it drop to the floor among the fast-food bags and abandoned newspapers. She'd grown to despise the tube in the two years she'd worked in the shop. A shop assistant. How did it happen? Why? Two years at drama school. Two on the boards. Two in a shop. And another birthday in June. She didn't even bother to read the trades anymore. Twenty-six. That's almost thirty. She'd be looking at comfy slippers next.

She picked up the piece of paper again. Richard. 7376 7377. Black jacket. Blue shirt. Dark jeans. Media: television, advertising, e-commerce.

The train pulled in at Hammersmith. As she stumbled along behind two girls in grey veils she thought about the crowd at Gloucester Road. Well-heeled. Closer to the action. London was a chessboard. Blacks and voids.

As soon as she got home she spread the slip of paper flat on the kitchen counter. She called the number. She let it ring twice. Then hung up.

It was ridiculous to call a total stranger. Then, it was ridiculous not to. What did she have to lose? She lit a cigarette and poured a glass of wine. The first drag and the first sip are the best. Life's like that. An unfulfilled promise. She'd played at the Royal Court in Sloane Square when she was nineteen. She was Polly in *The Raw Edge*, a pilot for a soap that had never got made. There had been hundreds of girls up for it. But she'd got the part. At twenty she could play fifteen. They liked that. She looked like the girl next door who gets raped and murdered.

She lifted the receiver and phoned again. Her sister.

'Alison. It's me.'

They talked: Alison's child. Alison's partner. Alison's stiff joints; she was learning to be a yoga teacher. Alison was about to hang up. Then remembered.

'How's things with you?'

'A man gave me his telephone number on the tube.'

'How exciting.'

'I know.' She paused.

'Well?'

'Nothing. He was a stranger.'

'What was he like?'

'Mmm. Tall, dark, nice accent.'

'Lucky devil.'

They talked some more. Said goodbye.

She finished her wine and started to pour a second glass, stopping herself and adding just a touch. She had decided to make the call while Alison was going on about her aches and pains and was bracing herself to actually do it. What would she say? What if she got an answerphone? No problem. She'd hang up.

There was no answerphone. He answered.

'It's me.'

'I knew you'd call.'

'How?'

'Nothing ventured. . .' He trailed off. 'Come over.'

'What for?'

'I could say a plate of spaghetti.'

'Why don't you then?'

'Okay. A plate of spaghetti.' She knew he was smiling. He gave her the address.

'Do you need to write it down?'

'I have a trained memory,' she told him.

'I'll put the water on.'

She replaced the receiver. This was insanity. He was an axe murderer. A madman. *American Psycho!*

It wasn't her that went through to the bathroom and took a shower. Shaved her legs. Perfumed her parts. It wasn't her. It was someone like her, a mirror image that stared from the mirror as she slid into black underwear. She cleaned her teeth. Lit a cigarette. Smiled at the absurdity of it. Of everything. She put on a black dress, looked down at her breasts, and took it off again. She tried blue jeans and a shirt. Good hips, she thought, took off the jeans and put on a skirt instead. Clothes help you find the character. Then, when you're up there, out there, you're no longer you, but then you are, even more so. Yes, they really were someone else's eyes peering back as she did her mascara. Someone who didn't work in the shoe department in a big store. She removed the skirt, slid back into the black dress, then swivelled round just quickly enough to catch a glimpse of Polly in *The Raw Edge*.

A taxi stopped as she was about to enter the tube and she stepped in the back. She despised London taxi drivers. But she loved their cabs. It was like returning to the womb. You were coddled; luxuriated. You learned how to love yourself, your reflection opaque and vaguely surreal in the dark glass, red and amber streaks of light crossing the sky. She imagined dying and being carried to her funeral in the back of a taxi. *Nirvana* on the radio.

He lived in a red brick building divided into five flats. His bell was the bottom one. She stood there on the threshold, her finger hovering before the shiny brass button. This really was madness. She marched off back the way she had come and only slowed her pace when she reached the newsagents on the corner. She studied the magazines. There was nothing she wanted to read. If she hurried she'd get home in time to see the movie on Channel 4.

She lit a cigarette and blew a long stream of smoke into the sky. The night was clear. Full of stars. She had every intention of going home and watching the film, but found herself crushing the cigarette below her heel, cleaning her teeth with her tongue, and setting out again for the red brick building.

She took a deep breath and hit the bell. The door buzzed open almost immediately. She heard his voice. 'Come in.' It was hollow. Like an echo. She heard the sound of her shoes tapping over the black and white tiles in the hall. There was a table piled with letters, a gilt mirror reflecting someone from the past.

Richard stood in the doorway to his flat. He was wearing jogging pants, a polo shirt. Bare feet. It's very familiar. Bare feet.

As she stepped into the hall he pushed the door just hard enough for it to catch. They stood motionless in the half-light. He leaned towards her, placing his two palms flat on the wall, her head trapped in the space between them. He wasn't smiling. He just stared. And she stared back. He had dark eyes. Jet black hair. She wondered if he would ever be cast as a leading man.

The slap stung her cheek. Loud in the silence. It was hard. Not so hard as to bruise, but hard enough for her teeth to cut the inside of her mouth. She tasted blood. She slapped him back, just as hard. Her breath caught in her throat. She would have screamed, but his lips were on her mouth, sucking at her and she responded to his kiss. His hands slid down the wall, across her back, over her bottom. He pulled up her dress and ripped the side of her knickers. They fell to her feet. She remembered reading in *Cosmo* that women got wet when they were excited. It had never happened to her. Never. But it did now.

She could feel a dampness inside her stomach. She felt that dampness grow liquid and leak from her, wetting her thighs. The feeling was . . . luxurious. The sound of the word ran through her mind as he turned her round and pulled her down on the floor. He entered her in one swift movement. The cheek where he'd hit her was pressed against the coarse floor covering. Her breath came in short little gasps. She could feel his breath, hot against her ear. He rammed deep inside her, harder and harder, and when he came the warm feeling in her stomach filled her whole body. I've been well and truly fucked, she thought. Luxurious.

Now that he'd finished she imagined he was going to open the door and toss her back out again. He turned her over and did something she had not been expecting. He kissed her cheek. He then lifted her awkwardly into his arms and carried her through to the bathroom. He didn't say anything. He turned on the taps, filled the big bath and added blue crystals to the flow. She was reaching for the zip on her black dress automatically, her fingers doing the thinking for her. He turned off the taps and she stepped into the foaming blue water.

He was about to go, but leaned back through the door: 'What kind of pizza do you like?' he asked.

'What about the spaghetti?'

'Takes too long.'

'Spinach with an egg.'

'Anything else?' he asked her.

'Yes, you can get this week's *Stage* at the newsagents.'

'You're an actress?' She nodded. 'I thought so. What's your name?'

'Greta May.'

'Nice one.'

He closed the door and she held her breath as she sunk for a moment beneath the dark blue water. Luxurious.

GRETA MAY

**Script/direction by
Clifford Thurlow**

**Produced by
Sacha Van Spall
and
Maureen Murray**

1 INT. THEATRE FOYER - EARLY EVENING

Greta May peruses the flyers in a rack. She is 25, pretty, down in the dumps.

Richard Bates, 30, attractive, quite confident, but not at all pushy. He carries *The Guardian* and wears a black shoulder bag. He recognises Greta.

Greta removes a flyer with a picture of a powerful handsome guy below the play title: *You're Not Alone.*

Richard approaches Greta, still with a puzzled look.

> **RICHARD**
> Hi, aren't you . . . you're Greta May.

> **GRETA**
> (*holds hands in surrender*)
> Afraid so.

> **RICHARD**
> I saw you in *Hope Express* . . .
> (*notices the flyer*)
> . . . with Oliver Morrell. Of course.
> That was something else.

> **GRETA**
> It was OK.

> **RICHARD**
> Amazing! What are you doing now?

                    GRETA
I'm sorry?

                    RICHARD
What are you in?
                    GRETA
I'm reading scripts, considering
a few things.
                    RICHARD
Wow. *Hope Express*. It had some really
Good ideas. Listen, do you want to have
a coffee or something?

                    GRETA
Another time. I've got to . . .
Greta moves past Richard.

                    RICHARD
Hey, good luck . . .

Richard scribbles his name and phone number on his
newspaper: *Richard 7177 7277*. He tears off the
corner and hurries after Greta.

                RICHARD (CONT'D)
Next time you're in something,
you know . . .

Greta reluctantly takes the scrap of paper.

Richard watches her meandering along the street,
shoulders slumped, and sees her drop the piece of
paper in the gutter.

2 INT. GRETA'S KITCHEN - NIGHT

Smoke spirals from an ashtray as Greta moves about
the kitchen. She gets a glass. Looks in the
fridge. There is a half eaten chocolate cake -

about four slices worth - which she puts on the table. She slams the fridge door.

She finds an open bottle of red wine in the cupboard and fills the glass. Greta gulps her drink. Wine drops in red tears down her front.

She sits studying Oliver's face on the theatre flyer, wipes away the wine with her fingers and real tears sting into her eyes…

> FLASHBACK
> There is a fleeting image of Greta dressed in an ultra sexy outfit consisting of a black bra and pants, teetering black heels and sheer black nylons held by suspenders. She looks terrified…

Greta's name called from offscreen shakes her from her reverie. She cuts and takes a big bit of cake. She toys with her mobile phone.

> **RACHEL (VO)**
> Greta. Greta.

Rachel Gold, Greta's flat mate, enters: same age as Greta, sexy in a slinky dress and ready for an evening out. She carries a necklace. Greta remains silent and looks shaken.

> **RACHEL (CONT'D)**
> You didn't get it...

> **GRETA**
> Perhaps I didn't want it.

Rachel gives her a long, hard look. Greta breaks off a piece of cake and shoves it in her mouth. Rachel glances at the flyer and puts it back on the table.

> RACHEL
> You know something, I've been dumped
> more times than you've had . . . hot sex.

> GRETA
> Some jerk gave me his phone number
> today, I mean...

> RACHEL
> Handsome jerk or an ugly jerk?

> GRETA
> You're so shallow. "Shallow Rachel!"
> It sounds like a play.

> RACHEL
> Yeah, I've seen it: It's all about a
> little girl who wants…everything, but
> the moment something goes wrong she
> wets her pants. Can you?

Rachel holds up the necklace. Greta stands to
help.

> RACHEL (CONT'D)
> So, what happened at the audition?

> GRETA
> They thought I was great.

Greta hooks the necklace in place. Rachel turns.

> RACHEL
> You didn't get it, did you?

Greta straightens Rachel's sleeve. She's looks
great. Greta looks sad. Rachel again grabs the
flyer, crosses the kitchen and drops it in the
bin.

>   RACHEL (CONT'D)
> Get over him. He's just a user.
> He used you. He abused you...
>
>   GRETA
> And he enjoyed it as well.
>
>   RACHEL
> Then you know what you have to
> do, Greta.

Rachel kisses Greta's forehead and makes her way
to the door. Greta sits and cuts into the cake.
Rachel turns and holds her own slender waist.

>   RACHEL
> Cake is not the answer.

Rachel closes the door. Greta speaks to the cake.

>   GRETA
> Depends on the question.

A door slams. Greta goes to the pedal bin, steps
on the pedal, and looks inside . . .

2A (Continues) INT. GRETA'S – KITCHEN – NIGHT

Greta sits, drinks, spins her mobile phone. She
stares thoughtfully at the keyboard, then stabs in
a number. It rings and she hangs up. She takes
another swig of wine, nibbles the cake, wipes her
lips with the back of her hand, streaking her face
with chocolate. She presses RECALL.

INTERCUT TELEPHONE CONVERSATION:

3 INT. RICHARD'S LIVING ROOM - NIGHT

Nice place.

> RICHARD
> Yeah...Richard.

> GRETA
> So what about that coffee?

> RICHARD
> What . . . Greta . . .

> GRETA
> You can tell me why Oliver Morrell
> was so *amazing* in *Hope Express*.

> RICHARD
> It's a powerful role. It's a good
> play. Yours was the more complex
> character…

> GRETA
> Why don't you tell me about it over
> That coffee?

> RICHARD
> Yeah . . . I'll give you the address.
> Have you got a pen?

> GRETA
> I've got a trained memory don't
> forget.

Greta listens. She goes to eat more cake, but
changes her mind.

4 INT. GRETA'S BEDROOM - NIGHT

Greta stands in front of the wardrobe mirror in modest underwear -

> *The same fleeting image of Greta dressed in the sexy underwear crosses the mirror and for a moment she sees Oliver behind her.*

She shakes away the image. Quick Cut to:

Greta dressed in blue jeans, tee-shirt and a leather jacket, hair carefully scruffy. She faces CAMERA and spins round to catch her reflection in the mirror - very James Dean with the fag in the corner of her mouth. *Nope.*

She wriggles out of her clothes and tosses them on the bed. She gazes at her image and combs her hair. She dresses in a formal suit - a demure Audrey Hepburn, and poses for the mirror. *Nope.*

Greta undresses and stands staring into the dark wardrobe.

Car lights flicker over the ceiling.

5 EXT. BLACK CAB - NIGHT

A black cab going West along Piccadilly, lights streaming by, Greta's reflection in the black glass flickers into a momentary flashback:

6 INT. THEATRE STAGE - NIGHT

Greta wears the sexy black outfit (from Sc. 4 flashback). She looks panicky as Oliver Morrell crosses a darkened room, empty but for the mattress on the floor.

Oliver slaps her across the face - he looks mean and enjoys abusing her. Oliver kisses Greta violently, and as she struggles to get away he pushes her roughly down on the mattress.

> GRETA
> You shit, what do you think
> you're doing? What the hell . . .

The voice of the dissatisfied Director intervenes from the darkened auditorium. We see now that the action is taking place on stage.

> DIRECTOR (VO)
> No, no, no, Greta, for heaven's
> sake…That was good, Oliver.
> Let's try again.

Oliver bends and touches Greta's shoulder in a sweet way. He raises his eye-brows as if to say he can't understand what's wrong with the Director and takes Greta's hand to pull her up from the bed. Greta smiles…

Close Up on Greta becomes her reflection in the cab window as the cab plunges into the tunnel at Hyde Park Corner and disappears.

7 EXT. RICHARD'S HOUSE - NIGHT

Greta's finger hovers over the doorbell: she is stunning in a black dress. The sound of a taxi disappears into a silence that is deep, oppressive.

Greta reads the name plate: Richard Bates. Her hand trembles, and she backs away. The cab has

vanished. Greta's shoulders drop. She dawdles
along the street in her heels, turns the corner
. . .

8 EXT. NEWSAGENTS - NIGHT

. . .and stops at the rack of magazines outside the
late night newsagents. It's gloomy inside, the dim
yellow light casting an insipid glow over the
pavement.

Greta pushes a cigarette into the corner of her
mouth. She is about to light up when she notices
The Stage, Screen International, Variety...She takes
The Stage out of the rack and flicks through the
pages.

She shakes herself and takes a deep breath. She
pushes the magazine back in place, removes her
unlit fag and stamps it out anyway.

9 EXT/INT. RICHARD'S HOUSE - NIGHT

As Greta marches back to Richard's building, she
opens her bag, removes the flyer with Oliver's
photo, tears it in half and drops the pieces in
the gutter.

Greta reaches the house and gives the bell a
decisive press. The voice on the speaker phone is
distant and hollow.

> **RICHARD**
> Hello.

> **GRETA**
> It's Greta May.

The door buzzes open. Greta enters the darkness. Richard is in an open doorway at the end of the hall in sharp silhouette with the light behind him.

10 INT. RICHARD'S LIVING ROOM – NIGHT

Greta stands with her back to the closed door in the living room. She is composed, ostensibly in control. Richard is in awe: Greta has become a sparkling femme fatale.

She studies Richard: his polo shirt, jogging pants, bare feet. She looks from his feet to his dark eyes and down to his feet again.

It's difficult to know who is going to look away first – but it is Richard.

> **RICHARD**
> What about that coffee?

> **GRETA**
> Red wine.

He digs in a cupboard and produced a bottle, glasses, corkscrew.

> **RICHARD**
> I didn't really think you were
> going to come. I mean, I'm glad
> you did . . .

He goes to clink glasses but she turns away at the last moment and slinks her way across the room to the gallery of photo frames.

> **GRETA**
> Don't they all come? The girls
> you give your number to...

The photos show: Richard as a little boy, in
school uniform, getting into a car, with mummy:
family snaps, all very normal.

> **RICHARD**
> I don't make a habit of it.

He approaches and Greta looks back at the photos.

Richard places his hand gently on her bare
shoulder, to point out something in one of the
photos.

> **RICHARD (CONT'D)**
> Look that was…

Greta flinches, as if she has woken from a dream,
and with the jerk of the movement red wine spills
down her front. Richard puts his glass down. So
does Greta. Her hand is covered in wine.

Richard goes to take her hand, and Greta slaps him
across the face in exactly the same way that
Oliver hit her on stage.

> **RICHARD (CONT'D)**
> What the . . .

As Greta goes to hit him again, Richard becomes
Oliver . . .

11 INT. THEATRE STAGE – NIGHT

FLASHBACK TO Scene 6:

. . .and Oliver hits Greta across the face.

He kisses her violently, and as she struggles to get away he pushes her roughly down on the mattress.

> ### GRETA
> You shit, what do you think
> you're doing? What the hell…No.

Oliver slides his belt out of his trousers and roughly ties Greta's hands. He hits her again. He is brutish and excessive

> ### OLIVER
> You're going to enjoy this, you
> little bitch.

> ### GRETA
> What? Why are you doing this . . .

> ### DIRECTOR (VO)
> He's not going to do anything.

The Director's voice brings the action to an end.

> ### DIRECTOR (VO, CONT'D)
> Ollie, a word please.

Oliver makes his way off stage.

The Director sits in an end seat beside the aisle, a ghostly figure in the dark auditorium. As Oliver approaches, the Director stands, but remains hidden, his voice like an echo inside Greta's head.

> ### DIRECTOR (VO, CONT'D)
> . . .I know you've worked together
> before, but this isn't doing it
> for me. I'm going to use the
> French girl . . .

The Director turns and his footsteps recede up the aisle. Oliver looks back at Greta for just a moment, then follows the Director.

Close up on Greta in the arc of a spotlight.

Close up on Richard, the lighting man behind the light.

12 RICHARD'S LIVING ROOM - NIGHT

CONTINUES FROM Scene 10:

Greta moves towards Richard, grips the side of his head, and kisses him. She kisses him harder, with such passion he stumbles backwards over a low chair and lands on the floor.

Greta falls on top of Richard, straddling him. She kisses his neck...she pulls off his shirt...as he goes to embrace her, she pushes his hands away.

The sex is fierce, noisy, violent. Greta is in charge. She has tears in her eyes.

Richard sees her tears. He slows the sex down.

>   **RICHARD**
>   It's okay . . .

She puts her hands over his mouth.

>   **GRETA**
>   Don't stop . . .

Richard caresses Greta. He gently rolls over and kisses away her tears.

Greta looks back at Richard as if she is truly seeing him for the first time.

13 INT. RICHARD'S BEDROOM - MORNING

Sunlight streams into the room. Greta is in bed wearing Richard's polo shirt. Her eyes slowly adjust to the light.

She snuggles up to Richard and the movement wakes him. He opens his eyes and they look at each other for a long moment.

> GRETA
>
> Where's that coffee you promised me?

Richard still can't quite believe she's there. He smiles . . .

> GRETA (CONT'D)
>
> Tell me what you thought of *me* in *Hope Express*.

> RICHARD
>
> You were adorable...

She pulls him towards her, pulling his ears, and kisses him tenderly.

> GRETA
>
> You know what I would adore: breakfast in bed.

> RICHARD
>
> With the papers?

> GRETA
>
> *The Stage. Variety . . .*

She stretches her shoulders like a cat.

Richard is about to get up, but she pulls him back.

                        GRETA (CONT'D)
          There's no hurry.

They kiss.

FADE OUT

Note

1. The quotations in this chapter from Sacha Van Spall are from an interview with the author.

Appendix 1: Glossary of Film Terms[1]

Above-the-line costs
The creative elements as detailed at the top of the budget sheet. Includes story rights and screenplay, producer and executive producer, director, principal cast and all associated costs.

ADR: Automated Dialogue Replacement, looping
Re-recorded dialogue to replace unfit recordings. Normally done back at a studio with the actors lip-synching.

AMPAS: Academy of Motion Picture Arts and Sciences
American professional honorary organization composed of over 6,000 motion picture craftsmen and women.

Anamorphic lens
A projection lens used to produce widescreen images at the cinema.

Ancillary rights
Rights to the commercial potential of a project aside from direct exploitation of the film. Includes computer games rights, television

spin-offs, prequels, sequels and remakes, book publishing rights, merchandising rights, soundtrack album rights, and the music publishing rights to the score.

Answer print
The composition print that emerges from the laboratory after the combination of the graded picture with sound, soundtrack and optical effects.

Aspect ratio
The width-to-height ratio of a movie frame and screen. Standard aspect ratio is 1.33 to 1; CinemaScope uses 2.35 to 1.

Audience positioning
The relationship between the audience and the media product. How the media tries to determine the response of an audience to its products.

Auteur
A film-maker, usually a writer/director, with a recognizable, strong personal style.

Backlighting
Lighting placed behind a subject to create a silhouette.

BAFTA: British Academy of Film and Television Arts
British professional honorary organization.

BBFC: British Board of Film Classification
The organization that issues certificates to films and videos, stating whether they are suitable for children or young people to watch.

Below-the-line Costs
The section of budget that includes technical, insurance, production, general expenses, editing and post-production costs.

Best boy
The chief assistant to the gaffer on a set.

Bollywood
The nickname of the Indian film industry (a mixture of 'Bombay' and 'Hollywood').

Boom
A movable arm that holds a microphone over actors' heads during filming.

Buzztrack, Presence, Atmos
Recorded atmospheric sound. The sound of silence. Also used as a backdrop for ADR.

CGI: Computer generated imagery
Used for everything from creating full on *Lord of the Rings* battle scenes to cleaning up minor details such as an errant watch on Napoleon's wrist.

Chain of title
The route by which the producer's right to use copyright material may be traced from the author to the producer through a 'chain' of assignments and transfers.

Chroma key
A device that allows an image to be filmed in front of a background that has been produced elsewhere.

Cineaste
A film or movie enthusiast.

Cinerama
A widescreen process using three projectors to produce an image on a curved screen.

CinemaScope
The trademark used for an anamorphic widescreen process.

Cinéma vérité
A style of film-making that stresses unbiased realism and often contains unedited sequences.

Clapperboard
A board on which details of each take are written in chalk, and which is 'clapped' in order to synchronize sound and vision.

Collection agent
A mutually agreed company appointed to collect the proceeds from a film and distribute to the financiers and other contractually agreed benefactors.

Completion guarantee
An agreement under which a guaranteeing company guarantees to financiers that the film will be completed and delivered by a given date.

Contingency
An amount added to the budget of a film to cover unforeseen circumstances, usually 10 per cent of the budgeted costs.

Continuity
Ensuring that each shot in a film or TV program has details that match.

Co-production treaty
An arrangement between two or more countries allowing film-makers to access tax incentives in each country.

Coverage
The shots, including close-ups and reverse angles, which a director takes in addition to the master shot.

Crane
A shot from above, using a device of the same name.

Cross-collateralization
Used by distributors and sales agents to apply costs from one territory or exploitation right to all other income revenues from all other territories and exploitations.

Cut
1. The instruction to stop the camera and the action in front of the camera.
2. The process of editing a film or shortening a scene.

Cutaway
A brief shot that interrupts the continuity of the main action of a film, often used to depict related matter or indicate concurrent action.

DAT: Digital audio tape
Tape used to store Digital recordings of a high quality.

Day for night
A shot filmed during the day, which appears on the screen as a night scene.

Deep focus
A cinematic technique whereby objects are kept in focus in both foreground and background.

Deferment
Payment from revenues derived from the exploitation of the film, after the deduction of distribution fees and expenses and, usually, after financiers have recovered all of the sums. Most short films are made with deferments.

Diagetic sound
Sound that belongs naturally with what can be seen in the picture.

Diffusion
The reduction of the harshness or intensity of light achieved by using a screen, glass filter or smoke.

Director's cut
The director's version of a film, which usually includes scenes cut from the original.

Dissolve
The gradual transformation of one scene to the next by overlapping a fade-out with a fade-in.

Distributor
Company responsible for the distribution and placement of a film in cinemas and other agreed media.

Dolby
A technique in sound recording that helps cut out background noise and distortion.

Dolly shot
A moving shot that uses a wheeled camera platform known as a dolly.

Domestic rights
The rights to distribute a film in North America or another originating country where specified.

DOP: Director of photography
The movie photographer responsible for camera technique and lighting during production. Also called the cinematographer.

E&O: Errors and omissions insurance
Insurance against claims arising out of infringements of copyright, defamation and unauthorized use of names, trade names, trademarks or characters.

Establishing shot
The first shot of a scene showing a wide shot of the location in which the action takes place.

Editor
The person usually responsible for the final structure of a film.

Equity
The British equivalent of the US SAG (Screen Actors Guild).

Fade-in
A gradual transition from complete black to full exposure.

Fade-out
A gradual transition from full exposure to complete black.

Film gauge
The size or width of film, e.g. 35 mm or 16 mm.

Final cut
The last version of an edited film prior to release.

Foreign rights
The opposite of domestic rights, the rights to distribute a film outside America.

Four walling
The renting of a cinema by a producer for a period allowing for the retention of all box office returns.

Frame/FPS frames per second
An individual unit of movie film. The American standard film speed is twenty-four frames per second; there are sixteen frames per foot of 35mm film.

Freeze-frame
A still picture during a movie, made by running a series of identical frames.

Gaffer
The main electrician and supervisor of lighting on set.

Gaffer tape
A strong and versatile multi-purpose cloth tape used for everything from marking floor positions to fixing equipment.

Gap financing
A lending arrangement whereby a bank will lend the difference between production finance raised and the minimum expected from sales by a reputable sales agent.

Gate
The part of a camera or projector in front of the lens, through which the film passes.

General release
The exhibition of a film that is shown in cinemas across a country.

Grip
A crew member who adjusts scenery, flags lights and often operates the camera cranes and dollies.

Gross participation
An arrangement whereby a participant in a film, usually a major artist, takes a share in the gross, rather than net, receipts.

Holdback
A period during which a particular form of exploitation is not allowed. An example would be a six-month holdback on video rentals to allow sufficient time for a theatrical release.

In-camera editing
A technique used when shooting on video. Requires shooting in sequence and re-recording over unwanted scenes.

Jump cut
A cut made in the middle of a continuous shot rather than between shots, creating discontinuity in time and drawing attention to the film itself instead of its content.

Key grip
The head grip who supervises the grip crew and receives orders from the gaffer.

Key light
The primary light in a scene.

Klieg light
A powerful carbon-arc lamp producing an intense light that is commonly used in film-making.

Laveliers
Small omnidirectional microphones usually attached to an actor's chest.

Loan out agreement
An agreement where the services of an individual are made available through a production company, usually owned or controlled by that individual.

M & E track
A mixed music and effects track, which is free from dialogue. Used for foreign language versions.

Master shot
A continuous take that covers the entire set or all of the action in a scene.

Matte shot
A partially opaque shot in the frame area. The shot can be printed with another frame, hiding unwanted content and permitting the addition of another scene on a reverse matte.

Minimum guarantee
The minimum sum a distributor guarantees will be payable to a producer as a result of the distributor's distribution of the film.

Mise-en-scène
From French meaning 'to put on stage.' The physical setting of the action and environment. It defines the mood, color, style and feeling of the world. It includes the style of art, camera movement, and lighting; architecture, terrain, atmosphere and color palettes.

Mix
To put together sound or images programs, or the sounds on a record.

Montage
The putting together of visual images to form a sequence.

Negative
An image that has been shot on to film from which a print or positive is taken.

Negative pick-up
A distribution agreement where the advance is payable only on delivery of the finished film to the distributor.

Net profits
The revenues from the exploitation of the film after distribution fees and expenses, deferments, repayment of any loans and investments raised to finance production.

Non-diagetic sound
Sound that does not come from anything that can be seen in the picture – i.e. the musical score or a voiceover (VO).

NTSC: National Television Standards Committee
A broadcast and video format using a fixed vertical resolution of 525 horizontal lines. NTSC countries are: the US, Antigua, the Bahamas, Barbados, Belize, Bermuda, Bolivia, Burma, Canada, Chile, Colombia, Costa Rica, Cuba, Dominican Republic, Ecuador, El Salvador, Greenland, Guam, Guatemala, Guyana, Honduras, Jamaica, Japan, South Korea, Mexico, the Netherlands Antilles, Nicaragua, Panama, Peru, Philippines, Puerto Rico, St. Vincent and the Grenadines, St. Kitts, Saipan, Samoa, Surinam, Taiwan, Tobago, Trinidad, Venezuela, the Virgin Islands.

Optical
A visual device such as a fade, dissolve or wipe, also includes superimposing and other special effects.

Option agreement
The right to exploit, during a specific period of time, for a specific sum, a book, screenplay, short story or contributors services for the making of a film.

Out-take
A shot or scene that is shot but not used in the final print of the film.

Overages
Distribution revenues payable to the producer after the advance or minimum guarantee has been recouped.

P & A commitments/spend
A contractual obligation imposed on a distributor to spend specified minimum sums on prints and advertising to support the initial theatrical release of a film.

PACT: Producers Alliance for Cinema and Television
The UK trade association for film and television producers.

PAL: Phase Alternating Line
Broadcast and video standard which is used mainly in Western Europe, Australia and some areas of Africa and the Middle East and provides a clearer image than NTSC. This standard is based on 625 horizontal scan lines and fifty frames per second. Used in Afghanistan, Algeria, Andorra, Angola, Argentina, Australia, Austria, Bahrain, Bangladesh, Belgium, Botswana, Brazil, China, Cyprus, Denmark, Ethiopia, Fiji, Finland, Germany, Gibraltar, Hong Kong, Iceland, India, Ireland, Israel, Italy, Jordan, Kenya, Kuwait, Lesotho, Liberia, Luxembourg, Malawi, Malaysia, Maldives, Malta, Mozambique, Namibia, the Netherlands, New Zealand, Nigeria, Norway, Oman, Pakistan, Paraguay, Portugal, Qatar, Seychelles, Sierra Leone, Singapore, South Africa, Spain, Sri Lanka, Sudan, Swaziland, Sweden, Switzerland, Syria, Tanzania, Thailand, Turkey, Uganda, the UK, Uruguay, Yemen, Zambia, Zimbabwe

Pan
A horizontal movement of the camera from a fixed point.

Pay or play
A commitment to pay a director or performer made before production commences, regardless of whether the production actually goes ahead.

Pitch
A verbal summary of a film delivered to busy executives; the *elevator pitch* gives the film-maker two minutes to tell his story and get backing.

Points
Shares of the net profits of a film, measured in percentage points.

POV: Point of View
A shot that depicts the outlook or position of a character.

Post-production
The final stage in the production of a film or a television program, typically involving editing and the addition of soundtracks. Also called post.

Pre-production
The planning stage of a film or television program involving budgeting, scheduling, casting, design and location selection.

Pre-screen
To see a movie before it is released for the public.

Press kit
An essential marketing document containing film-makers' contact details, film synopsis, behind the scenes production details, key profiles and photos, credits of key players, press clippings. Other handy tools: flyers, posters, stickers and business cards.

Producer
The person responsible for initiating, organizing and financing a venture.

Product placement
A form of sponsorship in which advertisers pay the producers of films to have characters use their products.

Recoupment order
The order in which investors and financiers are repaid their loans and investments.

Redhead
Standard type of lighting equipment.

Rush
The print of the camera footage from one day's shooting. Also called the *daily*.

SAG: Screen Actors Guild
American equivalent of British Actors Equity.

Sales agent
An agent appointed by the producer to act as agent for the sale of a film.

SCART
A 21-pin plug connector for audio and video between VCRs, camcorders and televisions.

Screenplay
The script for a film.

Scene
A succession of shots that conveys a unified element of a movie's story.

Sequence
A succession of scenes that comprises a dramatic unit of the film.

SFX
Special effects or devices used to create particular visual illusions.

Shooting script
The final version of a script with the scenes arranged in the sequence in which the film is to be shot.

Shot
The basic building block of film narrative - the single unedited piece of film.

Slate
The digital board that is held in front of the camera and identifies shot number, director, cameraperson, studio and title. The data was originally written with chalk on a piece of slate. This footage is used in the laboratory and editing room to identify the shot.

Soft focus
The device of shooting the subject a little out of focus to create a specific effect, usually to do with nostalgia, an attractive female star or dreams.

Sound stage
A soundproof room or studio used in movie production.

Source material
The original work on which the screenplay for a film is based.

SteadiCam
A hydraulically balanced apparatus that harnesses a camera to an operator's body providing smooth tracking shots without using a track.

Stop date
The last date on which a performer or director can be obliged to work. Allows an agent to schedule projects for a client.

Storyboard
The sketches depicting plot, action and characters in the sequential scenes of a film, television show or advertisement.

Sub-genre
A genre within a genre.

Sync
When sound and images are linked properly together in time.

Take
The filming of a shot in a particular camera set-up. The director usually films several takes before approving the shot.

Take-over
Completion guarantors and some financiers require the right to take over the production of a film if the producer becomes insolvent, or commits a material breach of his obligations to the completion guarantor, or if the financier encounters serious production problems.

Television rights
The collective expression for different forms of television, i.e. free and pay television, terrestrial, cable and satellite television.

Tilt
A vertical camera movement from a fixed position.

Time lapse
A technique of filming single frames of action at delayed intervals and replaying them at normal speed, to speed up dramatically an action or event.

Tracking shot
A shot that moves in one plane by moving the camera dolly along fixed tracks.

Trailer
A short filmed preview or advertisement for a movie.

Treatment
A detailed synopsis of a movie's story, with action and character rendered in prose form.

Turnaround
Occurs when an agreed period in which to put a project into production expires. The producer is entitled to buy the project back from the financier, usually for all or a proportion of the sums advanced by the financier.

Video assist/video tap
A junior assistant who relays images to a video monitor that allows the crew/director to check footage immediately.

Voice-over
The voice of an unseen narrator or of an on-screen character not seen speaking in a movie.

Wildtrack
A recording of background or atmospheric noise that can be used at the editing stage.
See also Buzztrack.

Note

1. Appendices: research by Sacha Van Spall.

APPENDIX 2: FILM FESTIVALS

There are now more than 2,000 film festivals world wide, and the number grows each year. Festivals used to be free. Most now charge for entry - anything from $10 to $50; the sky's the limit. Those that encourage mass applications may merely have found a lucrative way to finance their festival. Be warned, and be aware that research is the key to finding the right festival for a short film.

<www.withoutabox.com> is a good place to start. This US-based site facilitates registered members to apply to festivals online. Members can make as many applications to festivals as they wish (they still have to pay the entry fee, but Withoutabox acquires discounts at many festivals). At Withoutabox, film-makers can track their submission status, find fests that fit the film, even get email reminders for upcoming festivals. There is a message board for film-makers to network, and an online guide for creating a press kit.

There are innumerable festivals, but only prizes from the majors are going to help film-makers in their career. I have chosen a dozen of the best, eight in North America, four in Europe. (Short film and online festivals follow.)

Pick of the festivals

North America

Chicago Film Festival (October)
32 West Randolf St, Suite 600
Chicago, IL 60601-9803
Tel: 312 425 9400
info@chicagofilmfestival.com
<www.chicagofilmfestival.com>

Cinequest: The San José Film Festival (February–March)
476 Park Avenue, Room 204
San José, CA 95110
Tel: 408 995 5033
sjfilmfest@aol.com
<www.cinequest.org>

Florida Film Festival (June)
1300 South Orlando Ave
Maitland, FL 32751
Tel: 407 629 8587
filmfest@gate.net
<www.floridafilmfest.com>

Slamdance Film Festival (January)
5526 Hollywood Blvd
Los Angeles, CA 90028
Tel: 323 466 1786
mail@slamdance.com
<www.slamdance.com>

Sundance (January)
Salt Lake City, UT 84110-3630
Tel: 801 328 3456
programming@sundance.org

SXSW Film Festival *(March)*
1000 East 40th Street
Austin, TX 78751
Tel: 512 467 7979
sxsw@sxsw.com
<www.sxsw.com>

Telluride Film Festival (July)
379 State St #3
Portsmouth, NH 03801
Tel: 603 433 9202
tellufilm@aol.com
<www.telluridefilmfestival.com>

Toronto Intl Film Festival (September)
2 Carlton Street, Suite 1600
Toronto, Ontario MFB 1J3
Tel: 416 967 7371
tiffg@torfilmfest.ca
<www.e.bell.ca/filmfest>

Europe

Berlin Film Festival (February)
Potsdamer Stra 5
Berlin D-10785
Tel: 49 30 259 20444
program@berlinale.de
<www.berlinale.de>

Cannes Film Festival (May)
99 Boulevard Malesherbes
75008 Paris
Tel: 33 1 4561 6600
festival@festival-cannes.fr
<www.festival-cannes.fr>

London Film Festival (November)
National Film Theatre
South Bank, Waterloo
London SE1 8XT
Tel: 020 78131323
info@bfi.org.uk
<www.ibmpcug.co.uk>

Venice Film Festival (August–September)
Ca Giustinian
San Marco 1364-A
30124 Venice
Tel: 39 41 52 18711
das@labiennale.com
<website under construction>

Film Festivals for Short Films

(There are some repetitions with main twelve above; only websites
are listed.)

North America

AFI Fest
<http://www.afifest.com>

Anchorage Film Festival
<http://www.anchoragefilmfestival.com>

The Angelus Awards
<http://www.angelus.org>

Ann Arbor Film Festival
<http://aafilmfest.org>

Aspen Shortsfest
<http://www.aspenfilm.org>

Atlantic City Film and Music Festival
<http://www.atlanticcityfilmfestival.com>

Austin Film Festival
<http://www.austinfilmfestival.com>

Boston Film Festival
<http://www.bostonfilmfestival.org>

Chicago International Children's Film Festival
<http://www.cicff.org>

Chicago International Film Festival
<http://www.chicagofilmfestival.org>

Chicago Underground Film Festival
<http://www.cuff.org>

Cinema of the Spirit (Saratoga, New York)
<http://www.parabola.org>

Cinequest Film Festival
<http://www.cinequest.org>

Cinematexas Film Festival
<http://www.cinematexas.org>

Crested Butte Reel Fest
<http://www.crestedbuttereelfest.com>

Dances with Films Festival
<http://www.danceswithfilms.com>

Denver Film Festival
<http://www.denverfilm.org>

Fayetteville Film Fest
<http://www.fayettevillefilmfest.com>

Film Fest New Haven
<http://www.filmfest.org>

Florida Film Festival
<http://www.floridafilmfestival.com>

Fort Lauderdale International Film Festival
<http://www.fliff.com>

Gen Art Film Festival
<http://www.genart.org>

Hamptons International Film Festival
<http://www.hamptonsfest.org>

Hawaii International Film Festival
<http://www.hiff.org>

Heartland Film Festival
<http://www.heartlandfilmfestival.org>

Hollywood Film Festival
<http://www.hollywoodawards.com>

IFP Market
<http://www.ifp.org>

Johns Hopkins Film Festival
<http://www.jhu.edu/~jhufilm/fest>

Los Angeles Film Festival
<http://www.lafilmfest.com>

Los Angeles International Short Film Festival
<http://www.lashortsfest.com>

Lost Film Fest
<http://www.lostfilmfest.com>

Marco Island Film Festival
<http://www.marcoislandfilmfest.com>

Maryland Film Festival
<http://www.mdfilmfest.com>

Method Fest Film Festival
<http://www.methodfest.com>

Miami Film Festival
<http://www.miamifilmfestival.com>

Mill Valley Film Festival
<http://www.mvff.com>

Montreal World Film Festival
<http://www.ffm-montreal.org>

Montreal just for Laughs – Eat My Shorts
<http://www.hahaha.com>

Nashville Independent Film Festival
<http://www.nashvillefilmfestival.org>

New Orleans Film Festival
<http://www.neworleansfilmfest.com>

New York Underground Film Festival
<http://www.nyuff.com>

New York Film Festival
<http://www.filmlinc.com/nyff/nyff.htm>

NewFest: The New York Lesbian and Gay Film Festival
<http://www.newfestival.org>

Newport Beach Film Festival
<http://www.newportbeachfilmfest.com>

NoDance Film Festival
<http://www.nodance.com>

Palm Springs International Festival of Short Films
<http://www.psfilmfest.org>

Parabola Film and Video Festival
<http://www.parabola.org>

RESFEST Digital Film Festival
<http://www.resfest.com>

SXSW Film Conference and Festival
<http://www.sxsw.com>

San Francisco International Film Festival
<http://www.sffs.org/festival>

Santa Barbara International Film Festival
<http://www.sbfilmfestival.org>

Seattle International Film Festival
<http://www.seattlefilm.com/>

Short Shorts Film Festival
<http://www.shortshorts.org>

Slamdance Film Festival
<http://www.slamdance.com>

Slamdunk Film Festival
<http://www.slamdunk.cc>

St. Louis International Film Festival
<http://www.cinemastlouis.org>

Sundance Film Festival
<http://festival.sundance.org>

Swiss American Film Festival
<http://www.swisscinema.org>

Tallgrass Film Festival
<http://www.tallgrassfilmfest.com>

Taos Talking Picture Festival
<http://www.ttpix.org>

Telluride Film Festival
<http://www.telluridefilmfestival.com>

Toronto International Film Festival
<http://www.e.bell.ca/filmfest>

Toronto Worldwide Short Film Festival
<http://www.worldwideshortfilmfest.com>

Tribeca Film Festival
<http://www.tribecafilmfestival.org>

Vancouver International Film Festival
<http://www.viff.org>

WorldFest-Houston International FilmFestival
<http://www.worldfest.org>

Europe and World Wide

Berlin Film Festival
<http://www.berlinale.de>

Bermuda International Film Festival
<http://www.bermudafilmfest.com>

Brest Festival
<http://www.film-festival.brest.com>

Brief Encounters: Bristol International Short Film Festival
<http://www.brief-encounters.org.uk>

Cannes International Film Festival
<http://www.festival-cannes.org>

CineFestival
<http://guadalupeculturalarts.org>

Clermont-Ferrand Short Film Festival
http://www.clermont-filmfest.com
(biggest shorts festival in the world; full details listed under USEFUL
ADDRESSES)

Fresh Films Cologne
<http://www.short-cuts-cologne.de>

Copenhagen International Film Festival
<http://www.copenhagenfilmfestival.com>

Edinburgh International Film Festival
<http://www.edfilmfest.org.uk>

Flanders International Film Festival-Gent
<http://www.filmfestival.be>

Flickerfest International Short Film Festival
<http://www.flickerfest.com.au>

Greek and International Short Film Festival
<http://www.dramafilmfestival.gr>

Hamburg International Short Film Festival
<http://www.shortfilm.com>

London Film Festival
<http://www.lff.org.uk>

Moscow International Film Festival
<http://www.miff.ru/eng>

Oberhausen International Short Film Festival
<http://www.kurzfilmtage.de>

Raindance Film Festival
<http://www.raindance.co.uk>
(largest shorts festival in the UK)

Rotterdam International Film Festival
<http://www.filmfestivalrotterdam.com>

Rushes Soho Shorts Festival
<http://www.sohoshorts.com>

Venice Film Festival
<http://www.labiennale.org>

Vila do Conde International Short Film Festival
<http://www.curtasmetragens.pt>

Young Peoples Film and Video Festival
<http://www.nwfilm.org>

Online Film Festivals

Alwaysi
<http://www.alwaysi.com>

American Short Shorts
<http://www.americanshortshorts.com>

Big Film Shorts
<http://www.bigfilmshorts.com>

Bijou Café
<http://www.bijoucafe.com>

The BiT Screen
<http://www.thebitscreen.com>

DDPTV Weekly Film Festival
<http://www.ddptv.com>

DfiLM
<http://www.dfilm.com>

DiGiDance DiGital Cinema Festival
<http://www.digidanceonline.com>

Hollywood Shorts
<http://www.lalive.com>

ifilm
<http://www.ifilm.com>

Leofest
<http://www.leofest.com>

Manifestival
<http://www.manifestival.com>

New Venue
<http://www.newvenue.com>

Pitch TV
<http://www.pitchtv.com>

Reelshort
<http://www.reelshort.com>

ShortBuzz.com
<http://www.shortbuzz.com>

ShortTV
<http://www.shorttv.com>

Urbanchillers.com
<http://www.urbanchillers.com>

Yahoo Film Fest
<http://www.onlinefilmfestival.com>

Zoie Films Internet
<http://www.zoiefilms.com>

Australian Film Festivals

Cairns Film Festival
<http://www.filmfest.cairns.net.au>

Fitzroy Shorts
<http://www.fitzroyshorts.com>

Flickerfest
<http://www.flickerfest.com.au>

In The Bin Short Film Festival
<http://www.inthebin.net.au>

Melbourne International Film Festival
<http://www.melbournefilmfestival.com.au>

Newcastle Film Festival
<http://www.newcastlefilmfest.org>

Over the Fence Comedy Film Festival
<http://www.overthefence.com.au>

Port Shorts Film Festival
<http://www.portshorts.com>

Revelation Perth International Film Festival/Conference
<http://www.revelationfilmfest.org>

St Kilda Film Festival
<http://www.stkildafilmfestival.com.au>

Tropfest
<http://www.tropfest.com>

APPENDIX 3: USEFUL ADDRESSES

Academy of Motion Picture Arts and Sciences (AMPAS)
Academy Foundation
8949 Wilshire Boulevard
Beverly Hills, CA 90211. USA
Tel: 310 247 3000
ampas@oscars.org
<www.oscars.org>

American Film Institute (AFI)
2021 N. Western Ave
Los Angeles, CA 90027. USA
Tel: 323 856 7628
<www.afi.com>

Arista Development
11 Wells Mews
London W1T 3HD. UK
Tel: 020 7323 1775
arista@aristotle.co.uk

Arts Council
Visual Arts Department, 14 Great Peter Street
London W1P 3NQ. UK
Tel: 020 7973 6410
<www.artscouncil.org.uk>

Association of Film Commissioners International
314 North Maine, Suite 301
Helena, MT 59601. US
info@afci.org
<www.afci.org>

Ausfilm
FSA #12, Fox Studios Australia
38 Driver Avenue
Moore Park NSW 2021. Australia
<www.ausfilm.com.au>

Australian Centre for the Moving Image
PO Box 14
Flinders Lane VIC 8009. Australia
<www.acmi.net.au>

Australian Film Commission
GPO Box 3984
Sydney NSW 2001. Australia
<www.afc.gov.au>

Australian Film Institute
236 Dorcas Street
South Melbourne VIC 3205. Australia
<www.afi.org.au>

The Australian Screen Directors Association
PO Box 211
Rozelle NSW 2039. Australia
<www.asdafilm.org.au>

Australian Short Films.com
GPO Box 1426
Southport MC QLD 4215. Australia

BECTU (Broadcasting Entertainment Cinematograph and Theatre Union)
373–377 Clapham Road
London SW9 9BT. UK
Tel: 020 7346 0901
<www.bectu.org.uk>

British Board of Film Classification
3 Soho Square
London W1V 6HD. UK
Tel: 020 7440 1570
<www.bbfc.co.uk>

British Federation of Film Societies
Ritz Building, Mt Pleasant Campus
Swansea SA1 6EP. UK
Tel: 01792 481170
<www.filmsoc.org>

British Film Institute (BFI)
21 Stephen Street
London W1P 2LN. UK
Tel: 020 7255 1444
<www.bfi.org.uk>

British Universities Film and Video Council
77 Wells Street
London W1T 3QJ. UK
Tel: 020 7393 1504
<www.bufvc.ac.uk>

BritShorts (see below under Distributors)

Cineuropa (Italia Cinema S.r.l)
Via Aureliana 63
00187 Roma. Italy
Tel: +39 06 4200 3530

Clermont-Ferrand Film Festival
Festival du Court Metrage de Clermont-Ferrand La Jette
6 place Michel-de-L'Hospital
63058 Clermont-Ferrand Cedex. France
Tel: +33 473 01 65 73
info@clermont-filmfest.com
<www.clermont-filmfest.com>

Dazzle Films (see below under Distributors)

Directors Guild of Great Britain
15–19 Great Titchfield Street
London W1P 7FB. UK
Tel: 020 7436 8626
<www.dggb.co.uk>

European Coordination of Film Festivals
64 rue Philippe le Bon
B-1000 Brussels. Belgium
Tel: +32 2 280 1376
yblairon@eurofilmfest.org
<www.eurofilmfest.org>
(essential site for latest festival information)

Europscript
Suffolk House, 1–8 Whitfield Street
London W1T 5JU. UK
<www.euroscript.co.uk>

Fb Films
(movie-budgeting software)
<www.fbfilms.co.uk>

Film Distributors Association
(formerly the Society of Film Distributors)
22 Golden Square
London W1R 3PA. UK
Tel: 020 7437 4383

Film Finance Corporation Australia
GPO Box 3886
Sydney NSW 2001. Australia
<www.ffc.gov.au>

The Film Foundation
445 Park Avenue, Floor 7
New York
NY 10022. US
<www.film-foundation.org>

First Film Foundation
9 Bourlet Close
London W1P 7PJ. UK
Tel: 020 7580 2111
info@firstfilm.co.uk
<www.firstfilm.co.uk>
(supports short film-makers preparing to make their first feature).

The Global Film School
(professional internet training)
<www.globalfilmschool.com>

Inside Pictures
Kuhn & Co
42–44 Beak Street
London W1F 9RH. UK
Tel: 020 7440 5924
snuttall@kuhnco.co.uk
<www.inside-pictures.com>

Internet Movie Data Base
(The IMDB is an invaluable source of information containing credits
from virtually every film ever released.)
<www.imdb.com>

Kodak
(Always willing to cut a deal)

London Arts Development Fund
2 Pear Tree Court
London EC1R ODS. UK
Tel: 020 7608 6100
info@lonab.co.uk
<www.arts.org.uk/londonarts>

London Film and Video Development Agency (LFVDA)
114 Whitfield Street
London W1P 5RW. UK
Tel: 020 7383 7755
lfvda@lfvda.demon.co.uk
<www.lfvda.demon.co.uk>

New Producers Alliance
9 Bourlet Close
London W1W 7BP. UK
Tel: 020 7580 2484
queries@npa.org.uk
<www.newproducer.co.uk>

The Oscar Moore Foundation
c/o Screen International
33–39 Bowling Green Lane
London EC1R 0DA. UK
Tel: 020 7508 8080
<www.screendaily.com>

Panavision
(equipment hire)
<www.panavision.co.uk>

Producers Alliance for Cinema & Television (PACT)
45 Mortimer Street
London W1N 7TD. UK
Tel: 020 7331 6000

Raindance
81 Berwick Street
London W1F 8TW. UK
Tel: 020 7287 3833
<www.raindance.co.uk>
(incorporates the British Independent Film Awards; the annual festival is the largest showcase of short films in the UK; also makes shorts available on limited edition DVDs)

Rocliffe
<www.rocliffe.com>
('Connecting established industry to emerging writing and film-making talent.' Showcases short film-makers at BAFTA)

Screen International
(UK trade paper 'Updated around the clock from around the world.')
33–39 Bowling Green Lane
London EC1R 0DA. UK
Tel: 020 7505 8102
screeninternational@compuserve.com
<www.screendaily.com>

The Screenwriter's Store
Friar's House, 157–168 Blackfriars Road
London SE1 8EZ. UK
Tel: 020 7261 1908
info@screenwriterstore.co.uk
<www.ScreenwritersStore.co.uk>

Screenwriters Workshop
Suffolk House, 1–8 Whitfield Place
London W1T 5JU. UK
Tel: 020 8340 0261
<www.lsw.org.uk>

Script Factory
Linton House. 24 Wells Street
London W1T 3PH. UK
Tel: 020 7323 1414
general@scriptfactory.freeserve.co.uk

Script Tank
35c Alexandra Drive
London SE19 1AW. UK
ejeley@lineone.net

Senses of Cinema online journal
<www.sensesofcinema.com>

Shooting People
34 Keeling House, Claredale Street
London E2 6PG. UK
<www.shootingpeople.org>
(Internet community of film-makers)

Short Circuit (see below under Distributors)

Skillset (The Sector Skills Council for the Audio Visual Industries)
Prospect House. 80–110 New Oxford Street
London WC1A 1HB. UK
Tel: 020 7520 5757
info@skillset.org
<www.skillset.org>

TriggerStreet
<www.triggerstreet.com>
(Kevin Spacey's Triggerstreet provides a showcase for short films and uploaded scripts open to industry and public feedback. Three short film festivals are screened annually over the net with judges including Tim Burton, Cameron Crowe, Danny de Vito, Mike Myers, Ed Norton and Sean Penn)

UK Film Council
10 Little Portland Street
London W1W 7JG. UK
Tel: 020 7861 7861
<www.ukfilmcouncil.org.uk>

(Film-makers should apply directly to the partner organizations for funding. They can contact the Film Council by emailing: shorts@film council.org.uk with general enquiries about any of the short film schemes. *Contact names are correct at time of going to press.*)

London
London Film and Video Development Agency – Honnie Tang
Tel: 0207 383 7755
lfvda@lfvda.demon.co.uk
<www.lfvda.demon.co.uk>

Scotland
Glasgow Media Access Centre Ltd – Cordelia Stephens
Tel: 0141 553 2620
admin@g-mac.co.uk
<www.g-mac.co.uk>

East of England
Screen East – Nicky Dade
Tel: 01603 756879
production@screeneast.co.uk

East Midlands
EMMI/Intermedia Film and Video Ltd – Peter Carlton
Tel: 0115 955 6909
info@intermedianotts.co.uk

South of England
Lighthouse – Dean Howard
Tel: 01273 384222
film@lighthouse.org.uk

West Midlands
Screen West Midlands – Paul Green
Tel: 0121 643 9309
info@central-screen.easynet.co.uk

North West of England
Moving Image Development Agency – Helen Bingham and
Lyn Papadopoulos
Tel: 0151 708 9858
mida@ftcnorthwest.co.uk

Northern Ireland
Northern Ireland Film Commission – Andrew Reid
Tel: 028 9023 2444
info@nifc.co.uk
<www.nifc.co.uk>

North of England
Northern Film and Media
Tel: 0191 269 9200
info@northernmedia.org.uk

South West of England
South West Screen – Sarah-Jane Meredith
Tel: 0117 927 3226
sarah-jane@swscreen.co.uk
<www.swscreen.co.uk>

Yorkshire and Humberside
Yorkshire Media Production Agency – Chris Finn
Tel: 0249 2204
admin.ympa@workstation.org.uk

Writers Guild of Great Britain
15 Britannia Street
London WC1 9JN. UK
Tel: 020 7833 0777
<www.writersguild.org.uk>

Zoetrope Virtual Studio
<www.zoetrope.com>
(founded by Francis Ford Coppola in 1998 to launch the literary
magazine *Zoetrope:All-Story*, it has grown into a virtual studio with
facilities to upload scripts and a forum for producers willing to help
new writers get projects seen by the industry)

Zoo Cinemas
20 Rushcroft Road
London SW2 1LA. UK
Tel: 020 7733 8989

Short Film Distributors

United States

Apollo Cinema; Short Film Distribution
1160 Alvira Street
Los Angeles, CA 90035
Tel: 323 939 1122, Fax: 323 939 1133
<http://ApolloCinema.com>

AtomFilms
114 Sansome Street, 10th Floor
San Francisco, CA 94104
<http://atomfilms.com>

Big Film Shorts:
3727 W. Magnolia Blvd. Suite. 189
Burbank, CA 91505
Tel: 818 563 2633; Fax: 1 818 955 7650
<http://www.bigfilmshorts.com/home.htm>

IFILM
1024 N. Orange Drive
Hollywood, CA 90038
<http://www.ifilm.com>

Image Union
WTTW/Channel 11
5400 North St. Louis Ave
Chicago, IL 60625
<http://www.wttw.com/imageunion>

The Independent Film Channel
200 Jericho Quadrangle
Jericho, NY 11753
<http://www.ifctv.com>

Omni
PO Box 64397
Los Angeles, CA 90064
Tel: 310 478 4700; Fax: 310 478 7147
<http://www.omnishortfilms.com>

Seventh Art Releasing
7551 Sunset Blvd. Suite 104
Los Angeles, CA 90046
Tel: 323 845 1455; Fax: 323 845 4717
<http://www.7thArt.com>

Short Movies
1223 Wilshire Boulevard, # 421
Santa Monica, CA 90403-5400
Tel: 310 586 9678; Fax: 310 586 9688
<http://www.shortmovies.com l>

United Kingdom

Britshorts Limited
25 Beak Street
Soho, London W1F 9RT
Tel: 020 7734 2277
<http://www.britshorts.com>

Dazzle Films
The Impact Studios
12–18 Hoxton Street
London N1 6NG
Tel: 020 7739 7716
<http://www.dazzlefilms.co.uk>

Short Circuit
15 Paternoster Row
Sheffield S1 2BX
Tel: 0114 221 0569
shortcircuit@workstation.org.uk
<http://www.shortcircuitfilms.com>

France

Talantis
36 Rue Milton
75009 Paris
Tel: +33 (1) 45 26 13 02
<http://www.talantisfilms.com>

BIBLIOGRAPHY

Alpert, Hollis (1986) *Fellini, A Life*, Atheneum Publishing.
Baxter, John (1997) *Stanley Kubrick, A Biography*, Harper Collins.
Biskind, Peter (1983) *Seeing is Believing*, Bloomsbury Publishing.
Callow, Simon (1995) *Orson Welles, The Road to Xanadu*, Jonathan Cape Publishing.
Campbell, Joseph (1993) *The Hero with a Thousand Faces*, Fontana Press.
Crofts, Andrew (2002) *The Freelance Writer's Handbook*, Piatkus Publishing.
Eisenstein, Serge (1970) *The Film Sense*, Faber and Faber.
Field, Syd (1984) *The Screenwriter's Workbook*, Dell Publishing.
Field, Syd (1998) *The Screenwriter's Problem Solver*, Dell Publishing.
Fonda, Afdera (1987) *Never Before Noon*, Weidenfeld & Nicolson.
Freeman, D. J. (1995) *The Language of Film Finance*, Pact.
Frensham, Raymond G. (1996) *Teach Yourself Screenwriting*, Teach Yourself Books.
Gates, Tudor (1995) *How to Get into the Film and TV Business*, Alma House.
Gates, Tudor (2002) *Scenario, The Craft of Screenwriting*, Wallflower Press.

Gibbs, John (2002) *Mise-en-Scène, Film Style and Interpretation*, Wallflower Press.

Giles, Jane (2001) *A Filmmakers' Guide to Distribution and Exhibition*, Film Council.

Goldman, William (1997) *Adventures in the Screen Trade*, Abacus.

Goldman, William (2000) *Which Lie Did I Tell? More Adventures in the Screen Trade*, Bloomsbury.

Gore, Chris (2001) *The Ultimate Film Festival Survival Guide*, Lone Eagle Publishing.

Hammond, Paul (1997) *L'Âge d'Or*, BFI Publishing.

Hancock, Caroline and Nic Wistreich (2003) *Get Your Film Funded, UK Film Finance Guide*, Shooting People Press.

Houghton, Buck (1991) *What a Producer Does, The Art of Moviemaking*, Silman James Press.

Jones, Chris and Genevieve Jolliffe (2000) *The Guerrilla Film Makers Handbook*, Continuum.

Parker, Philip (1998) *The Art and Science of Screenwriting*, Intellect Books.

Thurlow, Clifford (2004) *The Sex Life of Salvador Dalì*, Tethered Camel Books.

Tobias, Ronald B. (1993) *Twenty Master Plots and How to Build them*, Piatkus Publishing.

Vogler, Christopher (1998) *The Writer's Journey*, Michael Wiese Productions.

Wells, Paul (2001) *The Horror Genre*, Wallflower Press.

White, Carol (1982) *Carol Comes Home, An Autobiography*, New English Library.

Steve Biddulph's quote on modern values (Chapter 3) comes from *The Guardian*, 11 December 2002.

Burt Lancaster's quote on directing (Chapter 3) is from a live interview at the National Film Theatre, 1988.

Sir Alan Parker – *Building A Sustainable UK Film Industry*, notes from a Film Council speech, 2002.

Alex Williams' quotes on *Gangs of New York*, *The Guardian*, 3 January 2003.

Index

239

Note: Index compiled by David Thurlow.